Life Is All About Relationships

© 2020 Leo A. Endel
924 17th St SE
Rochester, Minnesota 55904
laendel85@gmail.com

Edited by Lydia Allison Endel

Additional copies of this book
are available on Amazon.
ISBN: 9798558845662

Scripture taken from the Christian Standard Bible
© Copyright Holman Bible Publishers, 2017.

Cover photo credit to Diosming Masendo on Unsplash.
Cover people silhouette purchased from Forgiven Photography
through Lightstock.com.
Three Person Icon purchased from Lightstock.com

Life is All About Relationships

DEDICATION

To Sarah, my one
To Rachel and Lydia, our blessings
To my mom and dad,
my foundation and example
To Eric and Adam, my brothers
And to all who have been
a part of my life's journey.

And to Emmanuel Baptist Church
who has been my sounding board
for so many truths found in this book
Grace and Peace

And to the ultimate relationship
with God the Father,
my Savior Jesus Christ
and His Spirit at work in me.

TABLE OF CONTENTS

Life Is All About Relationships

Introduction

What is life all about? Most people don't ask the big questions about life and death until they look down into a six-foot hole and bury someone they love.

People spend more time evaluating the purchase of an automobile than they do considering what life is all about. For a moment, they consider the question at the death of close friend or family member, but grief leaves the mind foggy and the question is not seriously probed beyond the initial first weeks of grief.

Life's great questions stormed against me early. I lost an appointment to the Air Force Academy due to a knee injury in a high school basketball game. I was disappointed, but life went on.

July 11, 1979 started out just like any other day, but it became a day indelibly chiseled into my mind. It was the summer after my freshman year of college, and I was working with a guy who was rebuilding an old pipe organ in a small German town only 18 miles from where I lived. Mike and his wife Nancy picked me up sometime around 8:30 am. It was a gray drizzling day and we started north on a narrow hilly blacktop to Concordia, a road we had taken many times before. We were almost there when we approached the top of a hill; suddenly time stood still as we saw the car flash over the hilltop, on our side of the road, and slam head-on into us. What took only a second seemed to happen in slow motion.

I blacked out. When I came to, I could hear the steam hissing from the smashed radiators and the screaming of my friend who had been driving our car. His wife, Nancy was nine months pregnant riding in the front seat—I will not even describe what I can still see in my mind. I could not breathe, so I slipped the door handle forward and pushed open the door, reached up to the door frame and pulled myself up, then slumped over onto the ground in a puddle and could not move. Still fighting to breathe and realizing that I was now paralyzed from the neck down, I literally saw my life flashing before my eyes and thought I was about to die. I had a lot of regrets. Laying there in that puddle—19 years old—I faced death for the first time in my life.

Nancy died a few hours later. Her baby girl was dead before the paramedics arrived. Nancy was the first person I had known well who had died. In the months and years after Nancy's death, my faith was tested and deepened. Since that day, I have lost my grandfather, then at a very early age my dad, then all my other grandparents. Two years ago, my younger brother, Eric died. I have performed over fifty funerals. Death has constantly invaded my life, while I have friends who have not lost a single loved one well into their seventies.

Coming face-to-face with death jars most of us to reflect on what really matters. The cycles of modern life seem to leave little time for reflection. In life, we more drift through life's current than swim intentionally toward a destination. Some people entertain themselves until they die, never really thinking about the big questions of life. They quiet their minds with television, movies, entertainment, trips, alcohol and other drugs, sports, grandchildren... etc. Their busyness allows them to avoid deep reflective thinking. They've thought a great deal more about their hobbies than about eternity.

Last year I visited Westminster Abbey in London. The construction of the church building was begun in 1245 AD, and seventeen English monarchs are buried in the building today. The building, the glass, the art, the sculptures take us back almost eight hundred years. One gets the sense that people come and go but our buildings last forever, but actually, quite the opposite is true. Though the trees and mountains of this world seem permanent, they will all pass away. Only human beings will last forever. We alone were created for eternity.

I am now old enough to look back on much of my life and discover that the lessons of life come gradually. There are seasons in life in which we learn things by experience that we could not truly understand until we live through them. I look back on each decade of my life and think to myself, "I was so clueless!" I have learned to accept the truth that you cannot know what you cannot yet know. As Job put it, "Wisdom is found with the elderly, and understanding comes with long life" (Job 12:12).

Here is what I have learned. Our greatest longing is for physical, emotional, and spiritual intimacy. From creation we were wired for relationships; relationships are in our DNA. We can find this in God, we can find this in our family, we can find this in God's family, and we can find this in humanity, but all of life is really about relationships.

A man once asked Jesus, "Which command is the most important of all?" Jesus answered:

> Listen, Israel! The Lord our God, the Lord is one. Love the Lord your God with all your heart, with all your soul, with all your mind, and with all your strength. The second is, love your neighbor as yourself. There is no other command greater than these." Mark 12:29-31[1]

Popularly, this is summarized as "Love God and Love People." This summarizes all of God's law. When you let that sink in, you discover that life is about relationships. Life is about being rightly related to God and to each other. Life is about learning to love God and all others. A happy, fulfilling life is all about relationships

The Harvard Study of Adult Development has been gathering information on people throughout their entire adult lives in what some call the "Longest Study on Happiness." According to the study's current director, Robert Waldinger, one of their most meaningful findings

---

[1] All Scripture citations are from the Christian Standard Bible, (Nashville: Holman Bible Publishers), 2017, unless otherwise footnoted.

9

is this:

> "Those who kept warm relationships got to live longer and happier... and the loners often died earlier. Loneliness, kills. It's as powerful as smoking or alcoholism."[2]

George Vaillant, research director of the study from 1972- 2004 added, "The key to healthy aging is relationships, relationships, relationships." I'd say the same is true about the meaning of life; life is all about relationships, relationships, relationships!

I hope you'll stick with me on this journey. You can read this entire book in under five hours, but you may want to read it in sections. Thus the book begins with relationships grounded in the heart of God, explains what happened that broke our world, then traces our broken history, takes us to the cross of Jesus Christ, and then finishes with us in heaven as new and recreated beings to live in eternal joy and peace.

Life is about relationships, relationships, relationships!

---

[2] Liz Mineo, *The Harvard Gazette*, "Good Genes Are Nice, but Joy is Better", April 11, 2017.

GOD IS ABOUT RELATIONSHIPS

"In the beginning gods created the heavens and the earth." The opening words of Genesis are shocking when read literally. Further, many readers quickly gloss over the plurality of the words used for God, "Let **us** create man in **our** image..."

Yet, the oneness of God is stressed throughout the Old Testament. How can the opening words of the Torah begin with God in the plural? And yet, the Shema, so central to Judaism, stresses the oneness of God, "Listen, Israel: The LORD our God, the LORD is one." This oneness of God is one of the chief obstacles of a Jewish person acknowledging Jesus as God. Yet the Bible begins with a vague reference of what can only be fully understood in Christ.

Early Christian scholars examined the testimony of Jesus, in the light of the resurrection, and came to understand that Jesus not only claimed to be God, but that his resurrection had confirmed His claim. Those who had spent three years with Jesus clearly understood that Jesus was God in the flesh and then died for proclaiming their belief. The gospel of John begins with the great testimony that Jesus was the eternal Word of God. "In the beginning was the Word, and the Word was with God, and the Word was God" (John 1:1). Is it not interesting that John uses words that demand we look for the antecedent account of Genesis, "In the beginning God (God in the plural)?"

John's gospel forces us to come to grips with Jesus as God. Early theologians came to describe God's revelation in terms of what we now call the Trinity. God is one God in three persons.

Further, John's gospel gives testimony to the Father's interaction with the Son and the Spirit during Jesus' earthly life. What we see is God in constant conversation, God in relationship with Himself.

> The next day John saw Jesus coming toward him and said, "Here is the Lamb of God... he existed before me.'... And John testified, "I saw the Spirit descending from heaven like a dove, and he rested on him. I didn't know him, but he who sent me to baptize with water told me, 'The one you see the Spirit descending and resting on—he is the one who baptizes with the Holy Spirit.' I have seen and testified that this is the Son of God." John 1:29-34

Matthew gives a bit more information delineating the Father, the Son, and the Spirit:

> "When *Jesus* was baptized, he went up immediately from the water. The heavens suddenly opened for him, and he saw *the Spirit of God* descending like a dove and coming down on him. And a *voice from*

heaven said, "This is *my beloved Son*, with whom *I am* well-pleased." (Matthew 3:16-17).

> ## In the Trinity
> ### we see God in constant conversation,
> ### God in relationship with Himself.

Again, we see the Trinity in John 14:23-26 as Jesus is speaking:

> *Jesus* answered, "If anyone loves me, he will keep my word. *My Father* will love him, and we will come to him and make our home with him. The one who doesn't love me will not keep my words. The word that you hear is not mine but is from *the Father* who sent me. "I have spoken these things to you while I remain with you. But *the Counselor, the Holy Spirit, whom the Father will send in my name,* will teach you all things and remind you of everything I have told you.

Jesus' prayer in John 17 records a conversation between the Father and His Son. The passage is too lengthy to discuss fully in this book, but it is insightful. Jesus is speaking intimately to His Father about God's plan and purposes. He draws His disciples, and future disciples, into the intimate relationship circle of the Trinity. We catch a glimpse of the Trinity in relationship and a hint of how God desires to bring us into this eternal conversation.

May they all be one, as you, Father, are in me and I am in you. May they also be in us... I am in them and you are in me, so that they may be made completely one... (John 17:21-23)

> *God is in eternal relationship and conversation with Himself and is inviting us into this intimate circle.*

There it is again. God in conversation with Himself and the oneness of God... a oneness that somehow invites us into the intimate circle of the Trinity.

Relationship is at the core of who God is. He was not lonely when He decided to create us. He lacked nothing. He was in eternal conversation with Himself. This conversation is the foundation of all relationships.

As we will come to see later, God's character extends into the creation around us. Right and wrong are not arbitrary values, they are extensions of who God is. Lying is wrong because God is the truth. Murder is wrong because God is life. We were created to live in relationship just as God exists in eternal relationship with Himself.

Questions for Discussion

1. Why is it important to understand the Trinity in terms of relationship?
2. What are the implications of God as a relational being?
3. How has God built His relational attributes into humanity?
4. What does it mean to be invited into a relationship with God?

MANKIND IS ABOUT RELATIONSHIPS

> *"I see Jesus in every human being. I say to myself; this is hungry Jesus; I must feed him. This is sick Jesus. This one has leprosy or gangrene; I must wash him and tend to him. I serve because I love Jesus."*
>
> Mother Teresa

When two families brought their babies to our church, there was immediate interest, even delight in their faces when they met someone who looked just like them.

Our dog Bailey is a Golden Doddle (my wife would like me to add the adjective "beautiful"), she seems to know her breed. If she sees a dog that appears to be like her, she wants to connect.

As God displayed His glory in the creativity, the beauty, and splendor of creation, He finishes with His greatest accomplishment—a being fashioned to be like Him.

"Then God said, let us make man in our image, according to our likeness." Genesis 1:26

What is the image of God? To be completely honest, we are not sure. Genesis 1:26 uses two words to describe humankind: image (tselem) and likeness (demut). The word "image" conveys representation. The word, "likeness" means to be similar to. We represent God, and we are similar to God. These two words are again used in Genesis 5:3 to describe the birth of Seth. Every human being has been made in the image of God and made to be like God. John Piper has said, "Why did God create man? To show God."[3]

One of the practical implications of being created in the image of God is that all human life is infinitely valuable. We are valuable because we are created in the image of God. This includes:

the unborn
the poor and homeless
the racially different
the physically disabled
the mentally ill
the elderly
the criminals
even our enemies

---

[3] John Piper, Sermon, Created in God's Image, March 15, 2015,
https://www.youtube.com/watch?v=_qP2hAVR7EY

> *Disrespect toward any human being*
> *is disrespect to God.*

So many things hinder us from seeing God's image in every person we meet: pride, prejudice, misunderstanding, anger, jealousy, greed... etc. Our personal sinfulness has blurred the image of God in us. We declare His glory, but our likeness has been distorted by sin.

Why does the image of God include male and female? A careful reading of Genesis 1:27 is revealing:

> So God created man in his own image; he created him [singular] in the image of God; he created them [plural] male and female.

There is a plurality of persons within the Trinity; there is a plurality of persons within humanity.

Theologians note that the persons of the Trinity have differing roles. Though each person of the Trinity is God, Jesus came to live, die, and be resurrected. The Spirit came to guide Jesus' followers into truth and to empower our witness to the world. They are equal but they serve different roles.

So too, men and women are equal but serve different roles. People once accepted that men and women were both equal but different. Modern humankind is losing touch with this reality. With the perception of gender identity, our culture defies biology. Can mental and scientific gymnastics redefine biology? Ten years ago, few thought it could.

Here's an example of how language is used today to confuse logic. "British Man Makes History by Giving Birth to a Baby Girl" said the headline.[4] Shocking! How can this possibly be? The bottom line is all about word redefinition. In the end we discover there really is no story to this at all. By contemporary definition, a transman is a biological woman. Thus, this "man" is biologically a woman.

A couple of years ago I went back and read George Orwell's famous book *1984*. He seems to have prophetically predicted the future using terminology such as: doublethink, memory hole, unperson, thoughtcrime, newspeak, thought police, and Big Brother. He describes a reality much like the one we are living in today in which we ignore reality and are coerced into nonsense.

An increasing number of people today think mankind is nothing more than a more highly evolved animal. They think we have no more intrinsic value than a salamander. Yet, three thousand years of Judeo-Christian history had transformed the world by giving value to every human being. What will the next hundred years look like when mankind is no longer recognized as having been created

---

[4] British Man, 21, Makes History By Giving Birth to a Baby Girl, The Sun, https://www.thesun.co.uk/news/3972232/britains-first-pregnant-man-gives-birth-to-baby-girl/.

in the image of God, and assumed to be purposeless and useless, even a liability to the world in which we live?

To contemplate the divinity and humanity of Christ is challenging. He is both God and the image of God (man). Christ's humanity is the perfect untarnished image of God.

We were created in relationship with God and for relationship with each other. In Christ, that restoration of relationship is accomplished both vertically (with God) and horizontally (with each other). We will not find joy and fulfillment until we reconnect relationally with God and with each other. We were created for this.

Three thousand years ago, the writer of Ecclesiastes struggled with the meaning of life. Most scholars believe the writer was King Solomon, the man known worldwide for his wisdom. Solomon looked at the world and found "absolute futility" (Ecclesiastes 1:1) "under the sun." He found life to be broken, possessions to be empty, pleasure to be fleeting, power to be impotent, wisdom to be foolishness, and popularity to be lonely. When he had examined all that the world had to offer, he was left with only one meaning that made sense, "Who can eat and who can enjoy life apart from Him [God]?" (Ecclesiastes 3:25). In the end, the writer had concluded that life's meaning is found in a relationship with God.

C. S. Lewis explains that we cannot find happiness and peace apart from God, for we are created for relationship with Him.

God made us: invented us as a man invents an engine. A car is made to run on gasoline, and it would not run properly on anything else. Now God designed the human machine to run on Himself. He Himself is the fuel our spirits were designed to burn, or the food our spirits were designed to feed on. There is no other. That is why it is just no good asking God to make us happy in our own way without bothering about religion. God cannot give us a happiness and peace apart from Himself, because it is not there. There is no such thing.[5]

We were created for relationships. We cannot find purpose, meaning, and happiness apart from a relationship with our creator.

Questions for Discussion

1. How are we relationally similar to God?
2. How do we reflect His glory?
3. In what ways have we not clearly displayed the glory of God?
4. How do we disrespect God by the way we treat others?
5. What differences are there between males and females?
6. How can we display well the image of God?
7. How does God restore the priority of relationships to our lives?
8. Why do we need God to be happy?

---

[5] C. S. Lewis, *Mere Christianity* (HarperCollins e-books), Kindle Edition, 50.

Mighty to Save

Everyone needs compassion
A love that's never failing
Let mercy fall on me

Everyone needs forgiveness
The kindness of a Savior
The hope of nations

Savior,
He can move the mountains
My God is mighty to save
He is mighty to save
Forever Author of Salvation
He rose and conquered the grave
Jesus conquered the grave

So take me as you find me
All my fears and failures
Fill my life again

I give my life to follow
Everything that I believe in
Now I surrender

Hillsong, Written by Ben Fielding and Reuben Morgan

SIN IS ABOUT BROKEN RELATIONSHIPS

Sin destroys relationships. Adam and Eve's rebellion and its resulting consequences have broken and marred our relationship with God and with each other. All human relationships have been damaged. We know the first sin as "the fall." As a result of the fall, the world we now live in is a broken world, and we are all broken people.

When I was in seminary, Jack MacGorman told our Greek class a story I have recalled as the "Smarter than Rats" story. MacGorman grew up in the colder climate of Nova Scotia, Canada with a wise and thoughtful father. One day, MacGorman and his dad came across the evidence of rats eating food in their storm cellar. They placed a trap with a lump of cheese. Sometime later, they came back and saw a gruesome scene. The rat had taken the bait and the trap had snapped across his leg. In desperation the animal gnawed its leg to get away, but ultimately died in a bloody mess. MacGorman could sense a sermon brewing in his dad, "Son, we'd better clean that up and reset the trap." His dad paused, "We'll never catch another rat if we don't clean the trap." He paused again, then dropped the teaching point, "Wouldn't it be nice if men were as smart as rats. Satan hasn't cleaned a trap since the Garden of Eden."

Purchased from lightstock.com, conceptualmotion

Indeed, since the Garden of Eden temptation, Satan's tactics have changed little. Like Adam and Eve, we know what God says, yet we believe we know better. In the end, we deny the Word of God, rationalize what we do, and suffer the consequences.

The fall has left us senseless and defenseless. We are all repeat offenders. There are billions of us wandering around the earth hurting ourselves and hurting others. Unchecked, unrepentant sin leads to greater and greater levels of damage and bondage. Pain and suffering are all around us, and eventually we die.

It is important to see and understand how relationships are at the center of everything that is broken. Adam and Eve immediately realize that something has happened between them; they are naked and have tried to cover themselves. Their innocence and transparency are gone.

Soon Adam and Eve realize that another relationship has been broken as well. They hear God walking in the Garden and instead of entering conversation with Him, they hide from Him. When God calls out to them, Adam responds, "I heard you in the garden, and I was afraid because I was naked, so I hid" (Genesis 3:10).

Adam then blames Eve for what has happened, but ultimately, he blames God, "The woman you gave to be with me—she gave me some fruit from the tree, and I ate" (verse 12). Finally, Eve blames the serpent. No one takes responsibility for their sin.

God tells Adam and Eve about the consequences of their sin. To the man, God says:

> The ground is cursed because of you.
> You will eat from it by means of painful labor
> all the days of your life.
> It will produce thorns and thistles for you,
> and you will eat the plants of the field.
> You will eat bread by the sweat of your brow
> until you return to the ground,
> since you were taken from it.
> For you are dust, and you will return to dust."
> Genesis 3:18-19

From these words we ascertain that all of creation fell. Abstract these key phrases to understand what has occurred.

- The ground is cursed (where once there was a perfect garden)
- It will be painfully difficult to raise food in this damaged world.
- We will die, "return to the ground." This was the fulfillment of God's warning that if they ate of the tree they would die.

> *We are broken people*
> *living in a broken world*
> *waiting for death.*

Human sinfulness has spoiled God's good creation. We now live in a world marked by "painful labor," alienation, and death. Sin literally unleased hell on earth. We are now broken people living in a broken world. We are in bondage to sin and destined for death. We can no more expect to break God's laws and not suffer than we can expect to break the physical laws of nature and not suffer.

But there is good news embedded into the Bible's account of the fall. There is a hint of evil's death in the crushed head of the serpent, and there is what appears to be a punitive action from God that in reality is designed to leave mankind with hope. God expels Adam and Eve from the garden and places a guard to keep them from finding their way back in, eat of the tree of life, and live forever alienated from God and each other.

While sin unleased hell on earth, Jesus will later conquer sin. In his death, Jesus paid the penalty for our sin. In His resurrection, Jesus conquered the consequences of sin. Paul puts it this way, "The wages of sin are death, but the gift of God is eternal life through Jesus Christ our Lord" (Romans 6:23).

WE ARE ALL BROKEN

Years ago, a guest stopped me after church and said to me, "I want you to know that I am not a sinner. I'm even better than you." I was speechless. Don't get me wrong, I was keenly aware of my own sins, but she was apparently completely unaware of at least one of her sins—pride. Sin comes in many different flavors.

Years later, I joined a couple in marriage at the church I pastored. They had both come from a tough background of sex, drugs, alcohol, and motorcycles. The marriage was an awesome event, they asked me to clearly present Jesus and His offer of new life. I did. On Monday, my wife ran into a lady who said with an upturned nose, "I saw all those motorcycles and those people at your church on Saturday." Sarah responded with a report about the amazing wedding. The woman responded with a crooked, pained smile, "Well, I guess those people need Jesus too!"

It turns my stomach to even remember that story from twenty-five years ago. Jesus loved the non-religious people. His harshest words were saved for the self-righteous religious people who did not know how deeply broken and far from God they were.

We are all sinners. The English evangelist George Whitfield once received a nasty letter accusing him of personal sin. Whitefield answered honestly, "I thank you heartily for your letter. As for what you and my other enemies are saying against me, I know worse things about myself than you will ever say about me."

As I reached my teenage years and started to flirt with alcohol and girls, I began to have nightmares of a day when everything I had done wrong became public. In a theater, every sinful act, every lie, every corrupt thought, and every wrong played out on the large screen for everyone to see. Ultimately, this embarrassment, and the cleansing grace of God, led to a change in my behavior. Unfortunately, my sins became less obvious, and to this day I appear to be better than I really am.

In many areas of my life I have learned to cover over the brokenness in my own heart. In my mind, I defend myself against critics without saying a word. I curse not with bad words but will a broken and frustrated attitude. I get frustrated, defensive, or afraid without ever saying a word. On the outside, I can look as clean as a Minnesota snow. On the inside, I know all is not well with my soul. Sin is rooted deeply in our souls.

You are not worse than the preacher. The reality is that we are all deeply broken. We are not the creatures God created us to be but are instead wounded caricatures of what God wants us ultimately to be.

WE WILL ALL DIE

We are all very much aware of our own impending death. God had warned Adam and Eve, "but of the tree of the knowledge of good and evil you shall not eat, for in the day that you eat of it you shall surely die" (Genesis 2:17). The implication is that had Adam and Eve not chosen to rebel, they would have lived forever. Of course, God knew they would rebel, and God had worked out a plan to redeem them from death. But God is absolute integrity, He would not act as if death were an alternative unless eternal life was an alternative as well.

I have been fascinated by scientific insights that our bodies largely rejuvenate themselves every seven to ten years. Our old cells are replaced by new ones. The process doesn't unfold evenly throughout the body and some areas of the brain never rejuvenate.[6] In this, I see evidence that we were indeed created to live forever.

In the fall, sin brought death that changed us at the core. Dr. Frisen, who discovered cell rejuvenation believes that the reason we age and ultimately die is because of "DNA mutations, which worsen as they're passed along to new cells over time."[7]

Could this also be an explanation of why the Bible reports that our early ancestors lived longer lives? Could it be

---

[6] Chris Opfer, *How Stuff Works*, "Does Your Body Really Replace Itself Every Seven Years?" https://science.howstuffworks.com/life/cellular-microscopic/does-body-really-replace-seven-years.htm
[7] Ibid.

that these "DNA mutations" took time to develop? This is speculation, but this we know, all of us will die. The good news is that God has, in Christ, made a way for us to live forever. We will discuss this concept later in the book.

PRIDE IS ABOUT BROKEN RELATIONSHIPS

A fifth grader came home from school, bubbling with excitement, after having been voted "Prettiest Girl in the Class." She was even more excited when she came home the next day after the class had voted her "Most Popular." But several days later, when she announced she had won a third contest, she was somewhat subdued. "What were you voted this time?" her mother asked. "Most Stuck-up,'" the girl replied.[8]

That's the way pride works! It rots us on the inside and alienates us from others. It destroys relationships.

The very first sin was an appeal to pride. Satan came to Eve and enticed her to eat of the tree, "...when you eat from it your eyes will be opened, and you will be like God..." (Genesis 3:5). Did you catch the appeal? "You can be like God." Accordingly, theologians often identify pride as the most serious of the seven deadly sins.

Culturally we are confused about the concept of pride. There is nothing wrong in a moment of accomplishment to "take pride" in what we have done—earned a degree, expanded our family, received a promotion... etc.

---

[8] http://jokes.net/shortteacherjokes.htm

However, if that pride becomes a lasting attitude, sin has snuck into the fabric of our life.

We use the term, "pride" in multiple ways that chart a spectrum from self-respect, to self-confidence, to narcissism, to arrogance. Think about the differing concepts this way:

1. **Self-respect.** We are created in the image of God and are valuable. Self-respect is not about superiority and is not sinful.
2. **Self-confidence.** We all have the capabilities to do things well. We have been taught and trained and it is not wrong to believe we can do something well and to "take pride" in our work. Self-confidence is not sinful.
3. **Narcissism.** Everything is about us. Everyone else is simply a tool for our satisfaction. This spectrum of pride is sin.
4. **Arrogance.** Exaggerates our importance. We want you to know that we are better than you, and we'll broadcast our superiority in almost any way we can.

In Romans 12:3, Paul warns us, "do not think of yourself more highly than you ought." That's great advice but let us not forget that Paul's advice comes in the middle of a chapter about relationships. He is saying to us that pride poisons relationships.

I used to think that I didn't have major problems with pride. In fact, I struggled more with a lack of confidence than over confidence. But a decade ago, after reading Blanchard and Hodges, *Lead Like Jesus,* I came to realize that fear can also be a prideful behavior. With classic pride, we want everyone to know we've got it all together—some think they do, others like me, are afraid people will discover that we don't have it all together. Thus fear, in this context, is really about protecting our image. Fear keeps us from being real with others and being able to have healthy relationships. Both arrogance and fear are pride.

NARCISSISM IS ABOUT BROKEN RELATIONSHIPS

Sin is an overfocus on self. Sin puts self at the center of our universe. As we became alienated from each other, we became the center of our own world. In not being able to clearly see the pain of another, we use people or manipulate people to get what we want. It doesn't matter how much we hurt them; we want what we want.

Like a baby, we think the world exists to meet our needs. Without any concern for others we cry, grasp, scream, and demand what we want without any regard for the effect that we are having on others. We become classic narcissists, in love with ourselves and living without regard to others. We will steal to get what we want. We will lie to get what we want. We covet the possessions of another. Life is about getting all we can get.

Jesus' words resonate against this struggle, "What does it benefit someone to gain the whole world and yet lose his soul" (Mark 8:36)?

C. S. Lewis wrote:

> "We must picture Hell as a state where everyone is perpetually concerned about his own dignity and advancement, where everyone has a grievance, and where everyone lives the deadly serious passions of envy, self-importance, and resentment.[9]

Rabbi Haim of Romshishok is credited with the classic picture of hell contrasted with heaven. In hell, people are seating at a huge table with generous supplies of food on the table, but the people are starving because the spoons are way too long to feed themselves. Across the hallway people in heaven are seated at an identical table with masses of food. Again, the spoons are long, but the people are well fed and happy. They are using the oversized spoons to feed the people across the table. Narcissism blinds us and plunges us deeper into emptiness. Sin ultimately robs us of the joy that comes through relationships.

THE DIVIDED HEART
IS ABOUT BROKEN RELATIONSHIPS

William Faulkner said, "The human heart in conflict with itself is the only thing worth writing about."[10] Sin not only broke our relationship with others, but its devastation is

---

[9] C. S. Lewis, *The Screwtape Letters: Annotated Edition (in the 1963 Preface)*, Harper Collins, 1996, 7.

[10] William Faulkner – Banquet speech. NobelPrize.org. Nobel Media AB 2020. Thu. 27 Aug 2020.
https://www.nobelprize.org/prizes/literature/1949/faulkner/speech/

much deeper, it broke every individual's heart. We are at civil war within ourselves. It is not just the classic picture of an angel on one shoulder and a demon on another, the reality is that we are internally broken. We simply are incapable of consistently rejecting wrong thinking and behavior even within ourselves.

Even the Apostle Paul experienced the battle that rages inside of us:

> For I do not do the good that I want to do, but I practice the evil that I do not want to do. Now if I do what I do not want, I am no longer the one that does it, but it is the sin that lives in me. So I discover this law: When I want to do what is good, evil is present with me. For in my inner self I delight in God's law, but I see a different law in the parts of my body, waging war against the law of my mind and taking me prisoner to the law of sin in the parts of my body. What a wretched man I am! Who will rescue me from this body of death? Thanks be to God through Jesus Christ our Lord! Romans 7:19-25

Only Christ can save us from our broken selves! We know we shouldn't say it, but we say it anyway. We know we shouldn't lie, but we do. We know we shouldn't look at pornography, but then we do. We know we should be faithful to our spouse, but then we flirt with someone else. We know we should be kind and compassionate, but we get impatient and angry. We know we shouldn't listen to the gossip, but we do. We know we shouldn't pass the gossip on, but we can't help ourselves. We know we should help someone financially, but we don't. We know we have what we need, but we're jealous when someone else gets a new car or a new house. We know we should talk with God, but we don't, and then we act more spiritual than we really are. We know we are not really what our Facebook profile paints us to be, but we post everything we can to make ourselves look good. Most of us know we are broken sinners; all of us are. "For all of have sinned and fallen short of the glory of God" (Romans 3:23). All of us!

Jeremiah wrote, "The heart is more deceitful than anything else, and incurable—who can understand it" (Jeremiah 17:9).

Jesus said:

> For from within, out of people's hearts, come evil thoughts, sexual immoralities, thefts,
> murders, adulteries, greed, evil actions, deceit, self-indulgence, envy, slander, pride, and foolishness. All these evil things come from within and defile a person." Mark 7:21-23

God gave us the law to help us clearly understand what is right and wrong, yet mankind could not consistently live out right and wrong because of our broken nature. We rationalize our sin and excuse ourselves.

Ezekiel prophesied that there was coming a time when God would help us overcome the civil war within us.

> I will give you a new heart and put a new spirit within you; I will remove your heart of stone and give you a heart of flesh. I will place my Spirit within you and

cause you to follow my statutes and carefully observe my ordinances. Ezekiel 36:26-27

With a new heart, then and only then can we live out the greatest commandment given in Deuteronomy 6:5 (the Shema) and restated by Jesus in Mark 12:30 and Matthew 22:37, "Love the Lord your God with all your HEART..."

Ultimately, we come to understand that we cannot do relationships with love and integrity, in part because, we cannot even calm the civil war within ourselves. We need Christ to give us a new heart.

> *If we confess our sins,*
> *he is faithful and righteous*
> *to forgive us our sins and to cleanse us*
> *from all unrighteousness.*
> 1 John 1:9

JEALOUSY IS ABOUT BROKEN RELATIONSHIPS

Aesop famously told this fable of two neighbors who came before Jupiter and prayed for him to grant their deepest desire. One man was full of greed and covetousness and the other man was full of envy. So, to teach them a lesson, Jupiter responded that he would double the request for each man's adversary. The greedy man prayed for a room of gold, but immediately his joy turned to grief when he saw his adversary celebrating two rooms of gold. The second man pondered the situation, he already had all the money he could spend. Then it came to him that he might pray to have one of his eyes poked out, which would leave the other man totally blind.

Jealousy causes us to do illogical and destructive things. It poisons our souls. We measure our success or failure on the basis of what we perceive another possesses. Jealousy can take our perfectly wonderful life and make it miserable.

> *Jealousy can poison*
> *even the best of relationships.*

The second sin mentioned in the Bible is Cain's killing of Abel. Cain makes an offering to God that is not acceptable; Abel's offering was received. Why didn't Cain just then correct his offering and make it right? Scripture tells us, "Cain was furious" (Genesis 4:5). God, in love, warned Cain against giving into his jealousy and anger, but Cain ignores God's warning, premeditates an attack, and then kills his brother. Cain gains nothing. His jealousy has aroused murder.

Jealousy is an insidious evil that arises from comparing ourselves to others and thinking that we have been shortchanged in some way. Why did he get the promotion? Why did she get the new car? Why don't I have as fine a home as you do?

Social media has amped up the temptation of jealousy. On a typical Monday, everyone's vacation and weekend pictures have been posted. Exotic places have been explored. The grandchildren are delightful. You get the impression that life is perfect for all your friends. Only you live in a "blah" world where life isn't freshly painted, and you haven't been to the Bahamas in the last week. Very quickly you can find yourself being poisoned by the green-eyed monster of envy. You are being overcome by an illusion.

Sin robs us of our ability to be content. We compare ourselves to others and become jealous of what they have. We lose our ability to enjoy what God has freely given to us. We imagine that we would be happier if we had as much as the guy across the street. In the process, our discontentment robs us of the good things we do have and poisons our ability to live with satisfaction and contentment. Nothing we can hold in our hands can replace the loss of these intangible possessions.

I am challenged by the ending of John's gospel. Jesus had just reinstated Peter. For each of Peter's previous denials Jesus had told Peter to "feed my sheep." Finally, he eludes to Peter's martyrdom. Peter turns and sees John and asks Jesus, "Lord, what about him?" In words I have used to interrupt my own jealousies and comparisons, Jesus says, "If I want him to remain until I come, what is that to you? As for you, follow me." The Lord knows what you need and what is best for you; trust Him.

TRIBALISM IS ABOUT BROKEN RELATIONSHIPS

Genesis shows us how quickly sin destroys human relationships. The progression starts with Adam and Eve's sin, which leads to family disintegration and murder, which leads to tribalism in the Table of the Nations in Genesis 10. By Genesis 14, four nations wage war against five other nations.

Through the Torah, God defined every human interaction and every relationship between priests and laity, clean and unclean, righteous and sinner, the old and the young, the rich and the poor, males and females, Hebrew and foreigner, those who worshiped Yahweh and those who worshiped idols.

Tribalism is the sense of belonging and loyalty to one's own group of people, coupled with a sense of otherness and hostility against outsiders. It can be summarized as, "Us versus Them."

Everything around us separates us. The color of our skin, gender, the nation we live in, the God we serve, politics, sexuality, economics, conceptions of justice, support of our social institutions, our special cause, or even the sports teams we root for.

Tribalism becomes the root of much sin. It creates rivalry. It overstates differences and embitters competition and comparison. By finding our identity in clusters of people who are like us, we find support and safety not unlike what is found in gangs. This seems to offer us security and belonging at a personal level but sets us up for even greater conflict on a societal level. Tribalism destroys the unity of humanity and becomes a bridge to hostility.

The Robbers Cave Study was conducted by social psychologist, Muzafer Sherif in the 1950s, who formed two separate groups of 12-year-old boys. All 24 boys had similar backgrounds: white, protestant, middle-class, two parent families.

Separately, he guided each group into developing their own identity and culture. They chose a group name and decorated their own shirts and a flag. They competed against each other and the winners were awarded prizes.

Finally, the two groups were introduced to each other in a series of competitions. It took little time before the two groups were at war with each other. Cabin attacks, threats, name calling, and other acts of aggression became the focus of each group. When the boys began to develop weapons and Sherif saw, "murder in the eyes of the children," he stopped the experiment.

What had happened? Though the boys were similar, they developed a group identity that separated them from the other group. Identity grouping can come about by ethnicity, race, religion, geography, political party, sexual identity, clubs, nations, lifestyles, or causes. Differences often result in tension and occasionally are exaggerated into hatred.

Politics will never heal this broken world. Economic development will never heal this broken world. Material wealth and prosperity will never heal this broken world. Peace treaties will never heal this broken world. Equality will never heal this broken world. We are too broken to be healed by human institutions and we are too broken to heal ourselves.

> *If we desire to understand the broken society around us, we need only to look inside us.*

We can work for greater understanding and build relationships that cross these boundaries and draw us together rather that apart. This is our Christian role in the greater society around us, but we must know that better organization, ideas and justice can be improved in this world, but the problems they address will only be completely repaired in eternity.

The good news is that God is working out His plan to heal us and to restore human oneness. Revelation 22:2 tells us that when God creates the new heaven and the new earth, the leaves from the tree of life "are for the healing of the nations." People from "every tribe and nation" will be one.

SOCIETAL DISINTEGRATION
IS ABOUT BROKEN RELATIONSHIPS

Collectively, individual sin evolves into social collapse. That's what happens in Genesis 4; we begin to see the multiplied impact of sin. G. K. Chesterton wrote, "What is wrong with the world? I am." If we desire to understand the broken society around us, we need only to begin by looking inside ourselves. Society is the collection of millions of sinners, broken individually, sinning against each other individually and collectively. Is it any wonder why societies are always on the brink of ruin?

Individual sin, by its very nature, is rebellion. Sin is self-centered and leads us to ignore the needs of others. It underestimates the impact of what seem to be insignificant decisions that compromise our integrity and eat incrementally into our souls. A single bite of an apple looks superficial until you understand that it was tasted in defiant rebellion against God. Insignificant as it seems, it led to the reign of death.

Mankind cannot solve this problem. Government cannot solve this problem. Without God's law we move toward anarchy or despotism. We are pulled toward no social control or a tyrant in control.

The book of Judges illustrates how sin evolves into individualism and anarchy. "In those days there was no king in Israel; everyone did whatever seemed right to him" (Judges 17:6). A thieving son and his apostate mother created their own god and way of worship. Out of nepotism, they appoint one of their own as priest. They have made their own religion, ignoring the LORD in an ultimate statement of rebellion and apostasy. Now each man's religion is of their own making; right and wrong are no longer established; God's people cease to be a people.

Contemporary American culture is experiencing societal disintegration barreling toward anarchy. "My right, my body, I do what I want to do." "You can't tell me what to do." "You do your thing; I'll do mine." "Who are you to say what's right and wrong." We are flirting with ideas previously unthinkable. Today, many are now arguing that a woman has the right to kill her baby even after the child is born. Indeed, in anarchy there is no right or wrong, only power—political coercion or intimidation.

Today we have gods and religions of our own making. We see ourselves as spiritual but not religious. We sense the spirit is real, but we do not want to be part of anything that might constrain us. No organized religion is going to tell us what to believe, so we choose from a smorgasbord of religious ideas. We like the concept of love from Christianity. We like the tranquility of Buddhism. We like what the Dali Lama says about happiness. We like the Hindu idea of reincarnation. We think Oprah has got it all together. In the end we have a piecemeal of religious philosophy that is incoherent and has no core. We hold a confluence of beliefs that appear to make some sense on their individual merit but often contradict each other. It is a system that doesn't work or make any logical sense. We find ourselves unable to define right and wrong, because without God, there is nothing but emptiness, illogic, and opinion. Only in God can we find the piece that holds it all together.

We have entered a time of personal anarchy giving rise to the polarization of nearly every moral and ethical issue. Our society is deeply divided about sexual ethics, gender identity, marriage, law enforcement, guns, the value of human life, abortion, euthanasia, global warming, legalization of drugs, politics, and religious liberty.

Though America is coming unhinged and society is moving toward anarchy, it is relatively easy to see the potential of a pendulum swing toward despotism. Various expressions of socialism or communism have revealed a path that starts with anarchy and ends with a strong man or small group that consolidates all power and authority in a totalitarian regime.

Historians look at the 1917 Russian Revolution and recognize that the timing for revolution was perfect. The government was increasingly impotent to control the fracturing of the nation. The nation was roaring toward anarchy. Into the political vacuum, Lenin and then Stalin took control. The pendulum ultimately swung to despotism when Stalin consolidated his power and ruled with an iron fist. As a result, an estimated 20 to 60 million people lost their lives.

We are in one of the greatest periods of societal collapse in American history! Some are arguing that we are on the verge of a civil war based on political, moral, social, and religious differences. In a society in which there are no accepted laws and everyone "does what is right in their own eyes," there is no real sense of identity, community, and relationship. There is no longer agreement on truth. Right and wrong have become opinions and political or military might will eventually be the measure of what is right.

Without God's law, society disintegrates. God knows a nation cannot survive without laws. As God prepared to build a nation out of his newly freed people, he gave them laws that would establish a just and stable society.

RACISM IS ABOUT BROKEN RELATIONSHIPS

Racism is so ignorant a concept as to be unimaginable. To make judgments about the value of people based on the color of their skin makes no logical sense. Imagine a movie highlighting a war sparked over hair color! The concept is so ludicrous that even the Marvel movies would dismiss the idea—and they have people running around fighting with hammers and spider webs!

In the summer of 1965, right before I started kindergarten, my family and I were living on a small Air Force base just south of Kansas City. It was hot, so my mom took my brother and I regularly to the public swimming pool to cool off. She was an avid reader, and there were life-guards present, so I am sure she watched me out of one eye and read out of the other. I came home talking excitedly about my English friend that I had met at the pool. A couple days later we were back at the pool and my mom discovered that my "English friend" was black. I have no idea why I thought he was English, but she thought it was hilarious!

I have often thought about this experience, not because I remember it, I don't; but because it has revealed to me several things later in life:

1) Little kids, largely, naturally connect. They do not see differences; they see a friend.

2) Kids do differentiate. Kids are not blind. They see skin color, hair color, size, weight, sex, culture...etc. clearly, but they see variety with interest.

3) Kids learn to discriminate through watching or listening to others. Kids will begin to reflect the attitudes of their parents and other influencers around them. Unfortunately, some of these voices will be poisonous.

4) Often these kids have their attitudes hardened through conflict. Conflict is a regular part of life. In conflict we often look for allies and begin to exclude the "other side." The result is that gangs exist even where there is little basis for differentiation.

5) All of us need to see conflict as an opportunity to confront sin and seek unity. Conflict can harden us, or conflict can be the first step to tearing down the "walls of hostility" (Ephesians 2:14).

6) Racism is a sin against the Creator God, who made us all who we are, and a sin against our brothers and sisters. Jesus came to destroy the power of all

46

sin. He alone can set us free from sin; that is why He came.

Dr. Martin Luther King, Jr., famously said in his, *I Have a Dream Speech*, August 28, 1963:

> "I have a dream that little black boys and little black girls will be able to join hands with little white boys and girls and walk together as brothers and sisters."

There is only one race—the human race. We are all made in the image of God. All of us are Sons and daughters of Adam and Eve. Racism is one of the most wicked tools through which people can tribally divide.

POVERTY IS ABOUT BROKEN RELATIONSHIPS

My dad was a low-ranking sergeant in the Air Force in a day in which that meant we had a place to live but not much else. Only the officer's kids had stuff. I remember those kids having nice bicycles, fishing poles, sports equipment, and dirt bikes. I remember them taking nice vacations and living in nicer homes, but for the most part, we really had what we needed. Usually, my mom worked part-time to help ends meet.

But that changed in 1972 when we moved from Fairbanks, Alaska to Sault Ste Marie, Michigan. In the process, the government decided that they had overpaid my dad. Mom and Dad had used what money they had to go see our families after three years in Alaska. When the financial crisis hit, we had almost nothing, and there were no jobs available to my mom or dad to help bridge the gap.

I remember making excuses when the church kids were going to go out for an activity that cost money. I remember not being able to afford school lunches. I remember the beans and rice that we ate at almost every meal because it was the cheapest thing mom and dad could buy to fill three hungry boys. It took a decade to recover from the dominoes that fell during those days. I think it almost killed my dad.

We thought we were poor, and compared to the people around us we were, but in the middle of those tough years I found out what real poverty looked like. We were living at Clark Air Force Base in the Philippines when I first saw deep poverty. Our church was half Filipino and half US Air Force. Our youth group sang in barrios in the rural areas that were poor, but the people were strong and industrious. They might have been materialistically poor, but they were rich in hard work and family.

I played high school basketball for the Wagner Falcons which meant that we traveled the island of Luzon to play other multinational schools—one of which was the International School in Manilla. The students at this school were the children of wealthy diplomats and industrialists. Because of the difficulty of travel, we played Friday night games and then again on Saturday morning, so we stayed in the homes of the opposing team's players.

On Friday night I went to my host's home in a chauffeur-driven long black limousine. We arrived at a magnificent home with an imposing marble entryway, wrap around staircases, a high vaulted ceiling, and an impressive ten-foot-tall fountain. This entryway was huge, sixty or so feet wide by a hundred feet long. The back opened into a horseshoe garden with a beautiful swimming pool. Behind the main house was my sixteen-year-old host's own personal living quarters—a separate house! The next morning, he opened his closet to choose from over fifty pairs of name brand basketball shoes. We went back into the main house for breakfast and the cooks and waiters waited silently on our every need.

After experiencing this opulence, we got back in the limousine and started our trip back to the school. In the sunlight, I could better see the estate where I had spent the night—unbelievable wealth on display! Not five minutes later, we transitioned out of the neighborhood and passed an enormous garbage dump the size of four city blocks. On it were scores of mostly naked children in tattered clothing, rummaging through the trash for food. The smell, but more so the contrast of wealth and poverty, made me sick to my stomach.

The Bible makes it clear that God never intended for the poor to struggle like this. The Hebrew people were told to leave the edges of their fields and vineyards unharvested for the sake of the poor and the foreigners living among them (Leviticus 19:9-10 and 23:22). This was part of God's way of taking care of those in need.

God spoke to His people in Deuteronomy 15:7-8, 10:

> "If there is a poor person among you... do not be hardhearted or tightfisted toward your poor brother. Instead, you are to open you hand to him and freely

loan him enough for whatever need he has... Give to him, and don't have a stingy heart when you give...

Clearly, God intended for those who had resources to help those who didn't. Even more than this, ignoring the needs of another human being insults God, "The one who oppresses the poor person insults his Maker, but one who is kind to the needy honors him" (Proverbs 14:31). Jesus spoke of our need to give help to the needy:

> Matthew 25:34-36, "Then the King will say to those on his right, 'Come, you who are blessed by my Father; inherit the kingdom prepared for you from the foundation of the world. "'For I was hungry and you gave me something to eat; I was thirsty and you gave me something to drink; I was a stranger and you took me in; I was naked and you clothed me; I was sick and you took care of me; I was in prison and you visited me.'

Ignoring the needs
of another human being insults God!

John writes of the impossibility of claiming to love God while not taking care of the needy among us.

> "If anyone has this world's goods and sees a fellow believer in need but withholds compassion from him— how does God's love reside in him?" (1 John 3:17).

Clearly, poverty around us testifies to brokenness within us. Poverty is a relationship issue.

MATERIALISM IS ABOUT
BROKEN RELATIONSHIPS

Someone has said, "We were created to love people and use things, but today we love things and use people." What a tragedy! We all know people who take better care of their cars than they do their children.

> *"We were created to love people*
> *and use things, but today*
> *we love things and use people."*
>
> Anonymous

We have so much stuff! Sometimes I think back to my childhood and remember my dad's possessions. He had his uniforms, a modest car, a few changes of clothes, his watch, a transistor radio, his wedding ring and a TV. That's about it. Our standard of living has increased dramatically in my sixty years. It is unimaginable what we own today, but does any of it make us happier?

Years ago, a friend told me that he was getting rid of all of his toys. He was tired of taking care of them. The reality is that we think we own stuff, but honestly, stuff owns us. I have watched people spend hours and days taking care of campers and boats that they use once or twice a year. We literally pour our lives into taking care of our stuff. Ravi Zacharias called money "congealed life." Think about it, we exchange our life for things. Worse than this, the accumulation of wealth and possessions is like running a race you cannot win. There is always a nicer car you could own. There is always a cabin somewhere we want to enjoy. There is always a bigger ring, a nicer watch...etc. Possession by possession we get a moment of joy and then gradually even more emptiness as we want something more.

> *We think we own stuff,*
> *but in reality, stuff owns us!*

Here's the thing, stuff does not bring lasting happiness. In fact, if our soul is owned by the stuff we possess, then we have little time to connect with people. Further, our fascination with things becomes a spiritual obstacle for us. Many of God's choice servants can handle wealth and still give their priority to God. Most of us probably can't. Jesus said in Matthew 6:20-24, "No one can serve two masters, since either he will hate one and love the other, or he will be devoted to one and despise the other. You cannot serve both God and money."

Greed is often fed by insecurity, such as a hoarder worrying about having enough toilet paper, or an insatiable desire to have more and better than anyone else. Greed delivers very little to the greedy and usually leads to greater and deeper levels of unsatisfied desire. Just as drinking salt water never satisfies one's thirst, greed leaves us hopelessly striving for something more. It is rumored that John D. Rockefeller, then one of the richest men who ever lived, was once asked, "How much money is enough?" Rockefeller reportedly replied, "Just one dollar more."

The Apostle Paul warns us about the danger of materialism. "For the love of money is a root of all kinds of evil, and by craving it, some have wandered away from the faith and pierced themselves with many griefs" (1 Timothy 6:10).

EXPLOITATION IS ABOUT BROKEN RELATIONSHIPS

Exploitation is about using people for our own benefit. The powerful and wealthy are often in positions in which they can use others to extend their power and wealth. People with influence and money can intimidate people who don't have the money or influence to defend themselves. I believe we have the best of legal systems in America, but I also know that a lack of money makes it difficult for many to defend themselves and stand up for their rights. People with money can hire the best lawyers; people without money often suffer the loss or lose even more by risking a lawsuit or being defended by inferior counsel.

Today we often think of exploitation as sexual enslavement or abuse, but people are exploited for cheap labor, as easy marks for greedy lenders, for drug dependency, over charging, or for any insufficiency to defend themselves from abusers who have wealth and power. We can even take advantage of our spouse or our family in ways that exploit their love for us.

Employers can exploit workers by not paying them a fair wage, or by working them so long and hard that they have little to give their families and cannot meet their own personal needs. Landlords can exploit renters by always taking the maximum price for their rental units, allowing their property to go unmaintained, and showing no mercy to people who temporarily need a helping hand.

Lovers exploit each other for sex, while gratifying their lust without a commitment to the person. Many times, both sexual partners are simply using each other never recognizing what they lose with casual sex. Even pornography is the exploitation of people who are entrapped into a system that takes their innocence and intimacy and ruins it by making it a commodity to be bought and sold. Sexual slavery is well documented throughout the world and here in the United States.

People can exploit you for your support as they seek to rise higher and higher in social stratification. They can use your ideas to rise in a company. They can exploit your friendships and your connections to meet their needs. Most of us have had friends and coworkers use us for their personal benefit. We know to some degree what it feels like to be exploited.

INJUSTICE IS ABOUT
BROKEN RELATIONSHIPS

Isaiah begins his writings, "Learn to do what is good. Pursue justice. Correct the oppressor. Defend the rights of the fatherless. Plead the widow's cause" (Isaiah 1:17). The Old Testament prophets powerfully argued for God's people to fight against injustice. A highwater mark of our responsibility is articulated in Micah 6:8, "He has shown you, O man, what is good; and what does the LORD require of you but to do justly, to love mercy, and to walk humbly with your God" (NKJV).

In the cause of civil rights and the destruction of racism, Dr. Martin Luther King, Jr. wrote, *Let Justice Roll Down*, based on Amos 5:24, "But let justice flow like water, and righteousness, like an unfailing stream."

God calls us to speak up for the disadvantaged. We need to do what we can to defend the oppressed. We often get so attached to a political party that we speak for the platform planks that we agree with and are silent toward those we disagree with. For years, a friend of mine fought within a political party for change. His appeal fell on deaf ears, but he continued to be persistent. Ultimately, he changed parties and began to speak against the planks he was opposed to. Most of us can identify with his experience.

I am often saddened by the political nature of our country. I have found it impossible to accept any one political position. I buy into an economic/political system because I believe in its basic principles, but I fully acknowledge the weakness of all human systems. Nearly always, I find myself adopting a system and working to alleviate its weaknesses or vulnerabilities. I believe in capitalism and believe the Bible teaches us to work for our living. However, I also believe that the Bible clearly teaches us of the evils of greed and materialism and that we should help meet the needs of the poor. These concepts are not opposites. Like the two gutters on a bowling lane, we need to navigate between two seemingly opposite truths to find the approach needed: fully to the left or fully to the right and you're in the gutter.

The issues of our day demand that we be people guided by God's justice. We must stand on what we know to be true from the Scriptures. We must fight for the lives of the poor, the unborn, the marginalized, the discriminated, the abused, the foreigner, and the powerless.

We must do as Micah 6:8 says:

> **Do justice** (do what is right)
> **Love mercy** (love to see mercy for all)
> **Walk humbly with our God**
> (submit to God's laws and guidance)

LONLINESS IS ABOUT
BROKEN RELATIONSHIPS

"The biggest threat facing middle-aged men isn't smoking or obesity. It's loneliness."[11] Many argue that our greatest need is for intimacy. Even our need for forgiveness is about finding intimacy with God and with each other.

Sin separated Adam from Eve, and therefore mankind, from God. The intimacy we were created for has been severely impeded. We were created for deep connections, but sin leaves us separated and lonely. We long for intimacy but we are friendless in a crowd, hungry for deep meaningful relationships.

According to Dr. Amy Banks, our brains are wired to connect with others.

> Neuroscience is confirming that our nervous systems want us to connect with other human beings. A good example of this is mirror neurons, which are located throughout the brain and help us read other people's feelings and actions. They may be the neurological underpinnings of empathy - when two people are in conversation, they are stimulating each other's mirror neuron system. Not only will this lead to movement in similar muscles of the face (so the expressions are similar) but it also allows each to feel what the other is feeling. This is an automatic, moment to moment resonance that connects us. There have been studies

---

[11] Billy Baker, "Middle-Aged Men Biggest Threat: Loneliness", Boston Globe (3/9/2017).

that look at emotions in human beings such as disgust, shame, happiness, where the exact same areas of the brain light up in the listener who is reading the feelings of the person talking. We are, literally, hardwired to connect.[12]

Researcher Daniel Goleman summarizes it this way:

"The most fundamental revelation of [the discipline of neurobiology is that] we are wired to connect. Neuroscience has discovered that our brain's very design makes it sociable, inexorably drawn into an intimate brain-to-brain linkup whenever we engage with another person."[13]

If we are wired to connect, but aren't connected to God or others, we feel an unfulfilled longing and are left empty and stymied. We need a friend; we need God to satisfy our loneliness.

Scripture speaks of the resonance and joy that comes with relationship. Proverbs 27:9, "Oil and perfume make the heart glad, and the sweetness of a friend comes from his earnest counsel."

Hebrews 10:24-25 speaks to church relationships that dispel loneliness and enrich our lives, "And let us consider how to stir up one another to love and good

---

[12] Amy Banks, M.D., instructor of Psychiatry at Harvard Medical School, "Humans are hardwired for connection", Wellesley Centers for Women, September 15, 2010.
[13] Daniel Goleman, Social Intelligence: The New Science of Human Relationships, (Bantam Books, 2006), Kindle Edition.

works, not neglecting to meet together, as is the habit of some, but encouraging one another..."

The Psalmist describes the goodness of close friendships, "Behold, how good and pleasant it is when brothers dwell in unity" (Psalm 133:1).

Jesus adds the truth that even multiplies this effect by reminding us of how He is with us when we gather together. "For where two or three are gathered in my name, there am I among them" (Matthew 18:20).

If you don't have a friend? Make a friend! Don't wait for someone to approach you; take the initiative. Invite someone for coffee or lunch after an activity. Pursue someone you think you could enjoy. Build a relationship and loneliness will disappear. Remember, life is all about relationships!

CONFLICT IS ABOUT BROKEN RELATIONSHIPS

Years ago, my little girls challenged me about using the word "idiot," so I decided to quit using the word. Primarily, I used it when another driver had done something, well, stupid. I stopped using the word after my youngest daughter, probably about eight at the time, turned to my wife and said, "There aren't as many idiots on the road when you're driving." Ta da!

I have thought a great deal about my Type A personality. "This is my road. How dare you think you can use this road when I'm in a hurry!" There's no doubt that my self-centeredness hasn't yet been burned completely away from my unsanctified personality. I'm working on it and making some progress, but I notice that the national election cycle produces great stress in my life. I found myself in conflict with almost everyone—even my wife doesn't always agree with me!

While there might be any number of specific pressures that affect our relationships with others, I think there are at least eight categories to think through when you find yourself in conflict with someone. Not every conflict will include every factor. The relative strength of each factor is important to understand and consider to lessen the tension and increase the possibility of resolving the conflict productively.

1. **My World view.** I hold a biblical worldview. I view life through the wisdom of God's Word. Fewer Americans view the world in this way. Frequently, I need to remember this.
2. **My Values.** Again, I try to align my values and morality according to the teachings of the Bible. Other people do not share my values; likely, they have values that make sense to them.
3. **My Personality.** All of us have differing personalities. As a rule, I love people and want to talk with people; I want to be agreeable, but I also have strong opinions. Many conflicts are largely the clash of differing personalities.
4. **My Mood.** All of us must acknowledge that our moods affect the way we interact with others. If we're in a good mood, we overlook issues with grace; if we're in a bad mood, we might be ready to do battle. Did a bad mood cause this rift?

5. **Importance.** How important is the issue? If the issue has little value, it's worthy of little effort. If the issue is extremely important, then it's worth the fight. Many of the things we fight about really do not matter.

6. **Relationship.** How close is the relationship? While I'm willing to state a disagreement with someone I don't know, I'm not likely to contribute hours to trying to resolve the conflict. It simply is not worth a fleeting relationship. However, if it's my wife or one of my good friends, the conflict needs to be resolved.

7. **Facts**. Facts are facts. Many people ignore facts and live by feelings or emotions. For some people, facts will resolve a conflict; for others, facts don't matter. They simply ignore facts because they don't conveniently fit their agenda. Some people will disregard the truth.

8. **Love.** Finally, regardless of the conflict, never forget to love people—even your enemies. Speak the truth in love. Love them enough to speak the truth, but don't be harsh. Be full of grace and truth.

Conflict is a continuous challenge to all of us. It is always helpful to remember the instruction of Romans 12:18, "If possible, as far as it depends on you, live at peace with everyone."

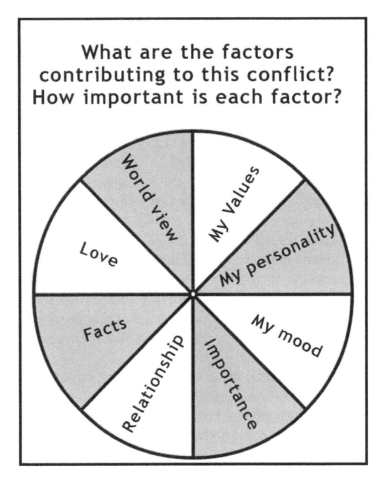

What are the factors contributing to this conflict? How important is each factor?

World view

My Values

Love

My personality

My mood

Facts

Importance

Relationship

Questions for Discussion

1. Why did God give Adam and Eve the opportunity to rebel against Him?
2. Who is responsible for the evil in the world today?
3. What were the relational consequences of the fall?
4. How did mankind change as a result of the fall?
5. Why did God lock Adam and Eve out of the Garden of Eden?

6. What are you doing to heal the effects of racism in your community?
7. How can you help the poor?
8. Are there things in your life that are more important than people?
9. What can you do to take a stand for justice?
10. Who do you know that is lonely and needs a friend?
11. What contributes the most to the conflicts you have with other people? Where are you broken?
12. What can we do today to bring healing to all this brokenness?

GOD'S GOODNESS IS ABOUT RELATIONSHIPS

We were both twenty-eight years old when our OBGYN doctor called us in to a conference. All I really remember was, "the recent tests reveal your baby will not survive more than a few minutes after birth." We were at full term and the doctor was correct, our child had tested positive for anencephaly. Nathan Allan Endel was stillborn with an underdeveloped brain. I still remember the emptiness as I walked through the same hospital doors, that days earlier, I had expected to excitedly exit carrying our newborn baby boy. The contrast was crushing.

To make matters worse, Sarah was terribly sick from the spinal block given during the birth. The doctor had determined her to be well enough to travel from Texas to Missouri for a graveside service. We purchased the airline tickets, but Sarah was physically very ill and showing no signs of improvement. Both of us were emotionally and spiritually struggling to make sense of what had happened. To this day, Sarah remembers little from the graveside service. I remember vividly my sick wife, the sleeting rain, and the cold weather. We sang, "It is well with my soul," but it was not well.

How could we come to grips with the facts? We were a young couple submitted to God's plan for our lives. We had left good jobs and traveled to Texas to prepare for ministry. We were excited about God's plan for us. We were two people trying to follow Jesus. We believed in the goodness of God, and then the bottom dropped out.

How could God, who has all power, not heal our baby? How could a God, who allowed this to happen, still be good? Theologians and philosophers call this perplexing question theodicy. Why do bad things happen to good people, or how can a good God allow so much evil in this world? This is both a complex and a simple question.

God created a "good world." Five times God pronounced each stage of creation good (Genesis 1). Finally, at the pinnacle of God's creation was His creation of humanity; God pronounced His creation as "very good." As we transition from Genesis 1 and 2 to Genesis 3, God's creation is perfect. He has created Adam and Eve and placed them in paradise under the most perfect of conditions, all is very good. But God's creation has one point of vulnerability. For Adam and Eve to be free to love God they must also be free to reject God.

God stacks the deck in Adam and Eve's favor and gives them only one command. They can do anything in the garden but eat from the tree of life. But like any preschooler confronted with a prohibition, they become fixated on this prohibition. Satan comes to them and plants doubt in the goodness of God (remember that God had again and again pronounced his creation "good" at the end of each day of creation). "Did God really say..." "You'll not surely die." "God knows that when you eat from it your eyes will be opened and you will be like God, knowing good and evil." Seduced by Satan's lies they believe God is withholding something good from them. They come to believe that God's commandments are not designed to protect them but to keep something good from them. They believe Satan's lie and eat from the forbidden tree—rebelling against the good God. Creation falls. God's good creation is broken.

> *What results from Adam and Eve's sin is not the world created by God, but a world spoiled by sin.*

What results from Adam and Eve's sin is not a world created by God, but a world spoiled by sin. God had warned them that eating of the tree would result in death. God's perfect creation is no longer perfect. Even weather, often explained as an "act of God" is a result of the fall. God's provision and mankind's innocence is lost. Everything has changed, and it was not God's fault.

Freedom to rebel was a necessity of creation. Adam and Eve were created to love God and to love each other. They could not truly love unless they could choose not to love. They had enjoyed intimate and personal conversation with God and each other, but their sin injected not only death, but fear and alienation into

God's creation. By the end of Genesis 3 everything has changed. The consequences of Adam and Eve's sin are pain, suffering, and never-ending toil. They pass from utopia into a life that is hard, painful, and ultimately ends in death.

Whose fault is this? God chose to give them the ability to rebel or they could not truly decide to love. Did God know that free beings would rebel? Yes. But God is not guilty for what mankind has done; we are.

The good news is that even in Genesis 2 God has an ultimate plan. Before the foundations of the world, God knew what would happen. He tells Satan that He has a plan to reverse the fall, "I will put hostility between you and the woman, and between your offspring and her offspring. He will strike your head, and you will strike his heel" (Genesis 2:15). The strike of the heal is not an ultimately deadly blow; the strike against Satan's head is. In time, this period of suffering will be overturned by God. He has a plan.

The last thing that happens in Genesis 2 is that God locks Adam and Eve out of the Garden of Eden lest they eat of the Tree of Life and live forever alienated from God and enslaved to sin. God is already working his redemptive plan.

In God's redemptive plan, God reverses the curse of sin and guilt when He comes to us in the form of His Son, Jesus Christ. God Himself comes to give Himself, as the only perfect sacrifice for the forgiveness of our sin. In His Holy nature He cannot look at sin and violate His goodness and His holiness. So, He offers Himself, He takes the ultimate punishment of death on Himself, so that as we identify with Christ by faith, His death covers our sin.

In Christ, we are forgiven. In Christ, God comes again to recreate a new heaven and a new earth where there is freedom but no sin. We will never again rebel against the goodness of God because we will unquestionably know the truth and the depth of God's faithful love toward us. We will once again celebrate His perfect creation in the new heaven and the new earth—heaven (Revelation 21-22). We will never again doubt the goodness of God, for we have lived through the rebellion that led to pain and suffering and we have experienced how deep and wide is the love of God (Ephesians 3:18).

Whatever pain and suffering we experience in this life, we can be sure that it is temporary. If we live to be one hundred years old, these days barely register in the light of eternity. Mankind has caused the pain; God has made a way to restoration and eternal peace.

The Apostle Paul adds this in Romans 8:23, "We know that all things work together for the good of those who love God, who are called according to his purpose." For those who have trusted in Jesus Christ for the forgiveness of their sins and for the reversal of the fall, God promises that even the painful experiences of life will ultimately work out for the good. Life might be painful, but it will ultimately be worth it.

In the end, our struggle in this world is about trusting the infinite God when we cannot understand the pain and suffering around us. My dad's favorite Scripture verse was

Proverbs 3:5-6. It has become my favorite as well:

Trust in the LORD with all thine heart;
and lean not on thine own understanding.
In all thy ways acknowledge him,
and he shall direct thy paths.

When my dad died at the young age of 59, we were devastated. Hundreds of his family, friends, and students gathered to honor him. Thinking about it now brings tears to my eyes. In the weeks and months that followed, I grieved. Sometime later, the students at the middle school where he taught sixth grade raised the money to put a polished stone memorial and a bench dedicated to my dad under the school flagpole. My dad's testimony still rings from the granite. Notice the Scripture listed.

When I heard about this generous act by my dad's students, I was taken back to the dark, cold day when Sarah and I buried our son. The very same words, "Trust in the LORD" (Proverbs 3:5), still settle me when I do not understand the pain in our world.

NATHAN ALLAN ENDEL
MARCH 24. 1988
TRUST IN THE LORD

The biblical book of Job is probably the oldest book of the Hebrew Bible. I have read the book many times and grown in my understanding of the book. Many things in the book sound true but God does not affirm them. God even refutes Job's friends and their arguments.

God allows Satan to test the godly man, Job. He accuses Job, and thus God himself, that Job's righteousness is but a façade for living a blessed life. His goodness is nothing less than a good business decision. If being good always leads to blessing, then any fool would be good. Doing what God said was right was not done to show one's love for God, but so that Job would have everything he wanted. Take it all away, said Satan, and the truth will reveal that Job is good because it pays to be good, not because he loves God.

God allows Satan to test his accusation on Job. Satan takes everything. Job loses his family, his fortune, his reputation, and finally even the support of his wife. He survives in abject pain and personal despair. His friends at first grieve with Job but ultimately, grasping to reconcile their righteous friend with the goodness of God, they defend God and condemn Job. Job knows he is innocent, and cries out to God in his pain, but he never denies the goodness of God.

> *God has a purpose for your pain.*
> *A reason for your struggle.*
> *A reward for your faithfulness.*
> *Trust Him and don't give up!*
>
> Anonymous

In chapter 40, God answers Job's questions not with neat theological answers but with His presence and a reminder that He is in control. Job can trust Him. Job humbles himself under God's word to him, then in response to the humble piety of Job's prayer for his friends, God restores Job's fortunes by giving to him double of everything Job had previously owned. Early in life, I noticed that God didn't double the number of Job's children—double donkeys but not double children. That does not sound right. Years later God brought light to the end of the story. Job lost his donkeys but not his children. Job's children we safely in the presence of God.

Things do not always look right "under the sun" (Ecclesiastes), but in the light of eternity we can trust the Lord.

Questions for Discussion

1. Is God responsible for all the evil we see in the world today?
2. Why doesn't God stop bad things from happening to good people?
3. How can we cope with the pain and suffering of this life?
4. Does it help to know that suffering in this world lasts for a brief time, but that our eternity will be forever perfect bliss?
5. Does God really understand our pain?
6. How has God entered into this broken world to help us get through it?

MARRIAGE IS ABOUT RELATIONSHIPS

Marriage is a three-ring circus: the engagement ring, the wedding ring and the suffering! For all of the jokes about marriage, most of us still want to marry our soulmate and build a life together.

Nothing brings joy to my life like my relationship with my wife, Sarah. We have supported each other through the pain, challenges, and joys of our life. From her have come our two greatest blessings, Rachel and Lydia.

Though relational fulfillment is not exclusive to the marriage relationship, Scripture supports the primacy of marriage as foundational to human relationships. Unfortunately, in our broken world not every marriage is a good one, and not every child grows up with a good mom and dad. Many children grow up with only one parent. But that was not God's plan; that is the result of the fallen human condition. God intended for marriage to bring joy and blessing.

The Bible presents to us three snapshots of marriage. First, there is marriage as God created it to be prior to the fall of mankind. Second, there is what I call broken

73

marriage that is the result of Adam and Eve's sin in the garden of Eden. Finally, there is what I call mended marriage in which God shows us how marriage can thrive even in this broken world between a broken man and a broken woman.

PERFECT MARRIAGE

Only Adam and Eve will ever know the utopian bliss of God's original plan for marriage, and we really don't know how long they experienced this bliss.

Marriage grows out of God's grand plan for mankind, male and female, being created in the image of God (1:27-28). I have long been fascinated by certain facts of the creation.

God reveals Himself in three persons, the Trinity.
The Father, the Son, and the Spirit are one.
They created the heavens and the earth.
God creates mankind in His image
Mankind is two persons, male and female
Male and female become one in marriage
They become co-creators in new life

It is worth noting that God created Adam and then noted, "It was not good for man to be alone" (Genesis 2:18). Man needed a partner, a helper, a complement. Though different in roles they would become one as cocreators with God in managing His creation. God's plan was for one man and one woman to be united for life.

The Apostle Paul notes that for the sake of the gospel, some people are gifted to depart from God's plan for the higher good of giving themselves for the sake of the gospel (1 Corinthians 7). Gifted to be single, these individuals are not second-class citizens in God's plan and Kingdom. Indeed, Jesus Himself never married; His life served a higher purpose. In many ways, single believers are specially devoted to God. Relatively few of us are called to this level of devotion, even Paul notes that for most people, marriage is God's plan (1 Corinthians 7:2).

There is compact wisdom contained in Genesis 2:24-26 that lays all future understanding of the purpose of marriage. Jesus Himself referred to this teaching when speaking about marriage.

> This is why a man leaves his father and mother and bonds with his wife, and they become one flesh. Both the man and his wife were naked, yet felt no shame. (Genesis 2:24)

I frequently preach weddings from this passage of Scripture because it is rich with meaning and insight. It reveals the heart of God in His good design for this most intimate of human relationships. These are a few of my main points.

Companionship in the Relationship
"It's not good for man to be alone..." (Genesis 2:18). I have often said that if you do not believe this, go and visit a college men's dormitory—it is not good for man to be alone. How wonderful it is to have a constant companion for life!

A Wedding Ceremony

Leo, will you have this woman to be your wedded wife, to love together after God's ordinance, in the holy estate of matrimony? Will you love her, comfort her, honor and keep her, in sickness and in health; and, forsaking all others, keep yourself only unto her, so long as you both shall live?
I WILL

Sarah, will you have this man to be your wedded husband, to love together after God's ordinance, in the holy estate of matrimony? Will you love him, comfort him, honor and keep him, in sickness and in health; and, forsaking all others, keep yourself only unto him, so long as you both shall live?
I WILL

I, Leo, take you, Sarah to be my wedded wife, to have and to hold from this day forward, for better, for worse, for richer, for poorer, in sickness and in health, to love and to cherish, till death do us part, according to God's holy ordinance; and therefore I pledge you my love.

I, Sarah, take you, Leo to be my wedded husband, to have and to hold form this day forward, for better, for worse, for richer, for poorer, in sickness and in health, to love, to cherish, till death do us part, according to God's holy ordinance; and therefore I pledge you my love.

With this ring, I thee wed, in the name of the Father and of the Son and of the Holy Spirit. Amen

Leo and Sarah, in as much as you have desired to be united to each other in marriage before God and these witnesses and have given and pledged your love to each other, I pronounce that you are husband and wife, in the name of the Father, and of the Son, and of the Holy Spirit. I present to you:
Mr. & Mrs. Leo & Sarah Endel
Leo, you may kiss your bride.

Help from the Relationship

"I will make a helper corresponding to him" (Genesis 2:18b). Marriage is a partnership of two people sharing the load of life together. Each brings to the marriage abilities and gifts that together enrich and sustain life. While marital roles certainly shift and adjust to the couple and their needs, both receive help from each other.

Primacy of the Relationship

"This is why a man leaves his father and mother... (Genesis 2:24). The Bible teaches us that we should honor our father and our mother (Exodus 20:12), but a married couple owe their primary allegiance to each other (Genesis 2:24). They are connected to the past but now press forward to the future. In this way, they grow together through life's challenges, and are sustained by each meeting the other's needs.

Permanence of the Relationship

"and bonds with his wife..." (Genesis 2:24). The word "bonds" indicates a permanent coming together. A modern paraphrase might be, "and is superglued to his wife." Never superglue anything together that you do not intend to stay permanently joined. Many of our modern glues are so strong that the glue joint is much stronger than the materials that are being joined together by it. To rip a glued object apart would result in permanent damage. This explains, in part, why divorce is so painful. Like two boards glued to each other the break is always ragged. You lose some of yourself as you are ripped apart in divorce.

Exclusivity of the Relationship

"and bonds with his wife..."

Bonding with your spouse leaves no room for another. If you are bonded to your spouse and have become "one flesh" together it is impossible to be one flesh with another. It is not logically possible.

We are living on the edge of seeing polyamory re-enter our culture. Some are already saying that the Old Testament affirms multiple marriages. The Genesis account shows that this was never God's intention. When we look at the Old Testament examples, all such relationships led to jealousy and pain. By the time of the New Testament, the Jewish people no longer practiced polygamy.

Intimacy of the Relationship

"And they become one flesh" (Genesis 2:24).

This is more than just the literal "one flesh" of joining two complementary bodies in sexual union. While this is part of the meaning of the text, it falls short of the full intimacy of the marital relationship.

Genesis 4:4, gives us a clue about the depths of this intimate relationship. "The man was intimate with his wife Eve, and she conceived and gave birth to Cain. She said, 'I have had a male child with the LORD's help.'" Genesis 4:1 The Hebrew word translated "intimate" is more literally, "knew." "Adam knew Eve his wife..." (KJV). Human sexuality was never intended to be a casual, physical encounter. Sexuality was intended to be the coming together of a husband and wife in the deepest of human commitment and physical pleasure—to know both emotionally and physically.

Procreation from the Relationship

"God blessed them, and God said to them, "Be fruitful, multiply, fill the earth and subdue it" (Genesis 1:28). God's creative plan was to allow humankind to participate in the stewardship of God's creation. He made the marriage relationship the cradle of procreation. From the marriage relationship would come other human beings created in the image of God to declare His glory and reign over creation.

Transparency in the Relationship

"Both the man and his wife were naked yet felt no shame" (Genesis 2:25). They were physically and emotionally free with each other. Without sin, there were no barriers, secrets, or defenses between them.

Innocence in the Relationship

"Yet felt no shame" (Genesis 2:25).
Prior to the corrupting influence of the fall (Genesis 3), Adam and Even were like unfettered children enjoying life together with no pain or shame. God designed marriage to foster the same kind of beautiful innocence between a man and a woman.

In the book, *The Case for Marriage*, Linda J. Waite and Maggie Gallagher write:

> A broad and deep body of scientific literature has been accumulating that affirms what Genesis teaches: it is not good for man to be alone—no, nor woman neither. In virtually every way that social scientists can measure, married people do much better than the unmarried or divorced: they live

longer, healthier, happier, sexier, and more affluent lives.[14]

God knew what He was doing when He created marriage.

BROKEN MARRIAGE

Most marriage jokes are brutal in their exposure of our idiosyncrasies and oddities. It is amazing how the one that dazzled us at the wedding now irritates us because they don't dispense the tooth paste properly. When two sinners come together in marriage, bliss takes work and sacrifice.

As we have noted, God's good creation was shattered by human sin. In Genesis 1 each day was pronounced "good" and when Adam and Eve were created, God pronounced it "very good." By the end of Genesis 3 everything is broken. This brokenness first appears in Adam and Eve's relationship.

Immediately these things happen:

- They realize they are naked (7-8), innocence is gone.
- They try to cover themselves and hide their loss of innocence and their rebellion (7).
- They hide from God (8).

---

[14] Linda J. Waite and Maggie Gallagher, *The Case for Marriage: Why Married People Are Happier, Healthier, and Better Off Financially,* (Chicago: The University of Chicago, 2002).

- They are afraid (10).
- Adam blames Eve.
- Adam blames God.
- Eve blames Satan.
- God covers their sin with the skin of an animal (horrible to two people born in innocence, one of whom had named the animals). We see much later that this covering of our shame would not be enough. God's ultimate act of dealing with our sin would be His covering us with the blood of His own son.
- God tells them the consequences of their sin.
- God expels them from the Garden lest they eat of the tree of life and live forever in their rebellious state.

The fall brings decimation to the individual and to all relationships—especially marriage. Where once there was intimacy between God and Adam and Eve, now there is alienation and strife. Women would desire relationships with their husbands, but sinful men would "rule over" rather than love them. God's plan for a beautiful relationship was seriously damaged.

We know from God's law, which was not yet available to Adam and Eve that, "Moses permitted you to divorce your wives because of the hardness of your hearts, but it was not like that from the beginning" (Matthew 19:8). The human heart is hard. Because of our sinfulness, some individuals will refuse to be true to their marriage vows. It is never God's plan for marriages to end. "God hates divorce" (Malachi 2:15), but we understand that it takes two people to make a marriage work—just one can walk away and end it.

The church continues to struggle with the complexities of broken marriages. In this fallen world there are few easy answers. Jesus made it clear that marital unfaithfulness allows for the dissolution of a marriage. Still, Jesus does not demand it, He simply allows it in these painful situations. God would still prefer that even devastated marriages be restored and be made right. It only takes one person to kill a marriage, so many times one partner is left decimated when they would have worked toward healing. For these individuals, divorce is thrust on them with little they can do to stop it. Though they may have contributed in some ways to the breakdown of the relationship, they are not the ones who walked away. They are left to rebuild their personal lives from the burning ruins of their home.

Don't give up too easily on your marriage. The Harvard Study of Adult Development has been gathering information on people throughout their entire adult lives. The study reveals that marital happiness declines dramatically with the birth of children and remains relatively low until they leave home, and then rises again.[15]

Research from the New Marriage Foundation reveals that "the majority of couples who are unhappy when their first child is born are happy ten years later if they stay together." Further, "Of parents who are unhappy at the time of the birth of their first child, seven in ten stay

---

[15] Robert J. Waldinger, The Study of Adult Development, Slide Presentation, Slide 20, http://hr1973.org/docs/Harvard35thReunion_Waldinger.pdf

together and of these the majority (68 percent) are happy ten years later."[16] Most marriages go through cycles, and if we persevere, we are happier again. These studies reveal that most of those who bailout on their marriages never find the happiness they are looking for.

A University of Chicago team study, led by researcher Linda Waite, uncovered these observations on divorce and happiness:

- Unhappily married adults who divorced or separated were no happier, on average, than unhappily married adults who stayed married.
- Divorce did not reduce symptoms of depression for unhappily married adults, or raise their self-esteem, or increase their sense of mastery, on average, compared to unhappy spouses who stayed married.
- Two out of three unhappily married adults who avoided divorce or separation ended up happily married five years later.[17]

Of course, these are statistical observations. While it takes two people to make a marriage work, one person

---

[16] Harry Benson, The Marriage Foundation, "For Better, for Worse: Staying in an Unhappy Marriage Could Be the Best Thing You Do" February 7, 2017. https://marriagefoundation.org.uk/wp-content/uploads/2017/02/Press-release-MF-Couples-on-brink.pdf
[17] Linda J. Waite, Don Browning, William J. Doherty, Maggie Gallagher, Ye Luo, and Scott M. Stanley, "Does Divorce Make People Happy? Findings From a Study of Unhappy Marriages", Institute for American Values: New York, New York, 2002. http://americanvalues.org/catalog/pdfs/does_divorce_make_people_happy.pdf

can destroy a marriage through abandonment, physical or emotional abuse, or unrepentant unfaithfulness. One person, attempting to uphold their marriage vows cannot save a marriage without the cooperation of his/her spouse.

The Apostle Paul writes in 1 Corinthians 7:15 of marriage between a believer and an unbeliever, "If the unbeliever leaves, let him leave. A brother or a sister is not bound in such cases." For many of us, this indicates the end of a marriage and the possibility of remarriage for the spouse who did not violate their covenant oath.

The death of any relationship can be a painful experience, but the death of a marriage can be the ultimate betrayal and one of life's greatest personal tragedies. God knows this, He expressed this pain in the book of Hosea in which God is presented as the faithful husband of an unfaithful wife. God knows the brokenness that comes in a broken marriage. He extends grace to the unfaithful partner who He hopes will repent. He gives grace to the wounded one endeavored to be faithful. God heals the broken hearted.

God heals the brokenhearted and bandages their wounds.
Psalm 147:3

MENDED MARRIAGE

We have already seen how the relationship between husbands and wives was damaged by the fall. God stepped in and gave the law as an imperfect remedy to the brokenness of human relationships. The law pointed to the coming of Jesus who would reverse the curse of sin and teach us a better way to live. I find it interesting that Jesus' first miracle occurred at a wedding!

In Ephesians 5, the Apostle Paul, shows us how to live out our faith in our human relationships. He is speaking to both the church and to marriage (5:21-33).

Our culture is stuck on Paul's "Wives, submit to your own husbands..." As a result, they never really understand the beauty and power of God's advice to married couples.

> ...submitting to one another in the fear of Christ. Wives, submit to your own husbands as to the Lord, for the husband is the head of the wife as Christ is the head of the church. He is the Savior of the body. Now as the church submits to Christ, so wives are to submit to their husbands in everything. Husbands, love your wives, just as Christ loved the church and gave Himself for her... In the same way, husbands are to love their wives as their own bodies. He who loves his wife loves himself.
> Ephesians 5:21-25, 28

Many years ago, a man called my office and begged me to meet with he and his wife. He had discovered that she was having an affair with her boss. She announced that she wanted a divorce and that she planned to marry her lover. Her husband was devasted. He admitted that he had neglected her and taken her for granted, but he was stunned. Though they were not members or attenders of our church I agreed to meet with them.

Among the many things we discussed was a side conversation from Ephesians 5—the "wives submit to your husbands" passage. We discussed the part of the passage that called for "husbands, love your wives, just as Christ loved the church and gave himself for her..." He hung his head low as he acknowledged his failure to love his wife in this way.

I felt prompted to ask her, "Would you submit to a husband that loved you like that?" She shot back with no hesitation, "Absolutely!" I was surprised; her husband was shocked! I thought we were near a breakthrough that might lead to repentance and restoration, but she could not believe it possible for him to love her that way. She filed for divorce, so that she could marry her lover. Her lover did not follow through and stayed with his wife and children. She lost her husband and the respect of her friends and family. Nine months later, she came by my office and thanked me for trying to stop her.

Looking at only one side of the marriage equation leads to a misunderstanding of marriage. When a couple clearly sees their own role and their spouse's role, balance comes into perspective. Too many couples insist on their individual rights rather than fulfilling their responsibilities to each other. When we serve each other, both husband and wife get what they need.

Put another way, selfishness destroys marriage, but sacrificial love will build a great marriage. Biblical submission is about a couple learning to serve each other by meeting each other's needs.

Often, God's wisdom seems counterintuitive to us. We resist his commands because we think we know better. He is imposing limitations on our freedom and our fun.

Emerson Eggerich notes that, typically, women desire love; typically, men desire respect.[18] The woman needs to be loved, so Paul commands the husband to love her and cherish her. The husband submits to his wife by loving her, nurturing her, and cherishing her. The husband needs to be respected, so Paul commands the wife to respect her husband. She submits to her husband by following his leadership and respecting him.

Eggerich has labeled these instructions as the Jesus roles:

Wives submit and respect your husbands.
"As Jesus submitted to the will of the Father" (Philippians 2:6-8). Wives let your husband be the team captain. Let him lead.

Husbands love and cherish your wives.
As Jesus loved and cherished the church.
"As Jesus loved the church and gave himself up for her" Ephesians 5:25. Husbands, give up your life serving your wife!

---

[18] Emerson Eggerichs, *Love and Respect: The Love She Most Desires; The Respect He Desperately Needs*, (Nashville: Thomas Nelson, 2014)

The husband's example is Christ, who took on human flesh and died for us. The husband's sacrificial love should never demand its own way. Sacrificial love puts the interests of the other ahead of its own. Thus, the husband is to nurture his wife by providing her with everything necessary for her to flourish. Paul is not primarily speaking of material provision as much as he is about nurturing her to fulfill God's greatest calling on her life.

Paul also adds that a husband is to cherish his wife. To cherish is to hold her close with warmth and tender love. In context it means to so value her that you always want what is best for her. Paul is telling husbands to serve their wife and their wife's fulfillment, not their own interests.

With great insight, Eggerich speaks of the Crazy Cycle of a relationship that spirals downward due to a lack of love from the husband and lack of respect from the wife. It might be more helpful to call it Crazy Love and put it this way:

> With love from him,
> She responds with respect.
> With respect from her,
> He reacts with love.[19]
> Together they experience crazy love!

In summary, a great marriage is built when a wife submits to her husband by following his leadership and respecting him, and a husband submits to his wife by loving her,

---

[19] A positive restatement of Eggerichs, 5.

nurturing her, and cherishing her. Amazingly, if this formula is followed, both the husband and the wife get what they need to the glory of God. That's a mended or healed marriage!

Throughout this passage of Scripture, Paul intertwines marriage between a husband and a wife with what Jesus has done for the church. The gospel becomes a metaphor for a healthy marriage. Both a healthy marriage and the gospel itself declare the glory of God.

SEX

Sex is God's idea. A friend of mine preached on sex and embarrassed his wife by adding the comment, "Yay, God!"

Human sexuality is one of God's greatest gifts, but as a result, it is often one of His most abused. The adage is correct: sex is like a fire. In the fireplace a fire is warm and pleasant; it is mesmerizing and wonderful, but if it is started in the middle of the living room it is devastating and destructive. Sex in the exclusive bonds of marriage is delightful. Sex outside of marriage is diminutive at best and devasting at its worst.

In Genesis 2:24, God speaks first about the purpose of human sexuality. "This is why a man leaves his father and mother and bonds with his wife, and they become one flesh." There is no more beautiful way of describing sexual intercourse: bonding and becoming one flesh.

Clearly, God intended sexuality to connect a man and a woman deeply and permanently. He even designed our bodies to connect more intimately in this act of love than in any other way. Sexual intercourse was designed by God to deepen our connection emotionally with our spouse.

In the words of the 12th century Jewish scholar, Nachmaides, God's plan for sex was holy. "Let the holy act be performed on the holy day."[20] The Mishnah Torah, Shabbat 30:14, puts it this way, "Sexual relations are considered a dimension of Sabbath pleasure." Make that statement a part of your church's website; I guarantee you will find more people interested in following God's biblical plan!

> *"Let the holy act*
> *be performed on the holy day."*
> Nachmaides

God intended for sex to be a part of the bonding between a husband and a wife. Sex is a connection that ties a man to his wife and a woman to her husband. In the bonds of marriage, this pulls a couple together through the trials and challenges of life. They nurture each other, they comfort each other, they bring pleasure and joy to each other in the harshness of life.

---

[20] Benjamin Blech, *The Idiot's Guide to Jewish History and Culture*, (Indianapolis: Alpha Books A Pearson Education Company, 1999), 17.

Russell Moore, in his book, *Sexual Brokenness and the Hope of the Gospel*, describes ways we are sexually broken and the damage that comes as a result:

> Having multiple sexual partners when you are young actually rewires your brain in a way that makes genuine, lasting selfless relationships much more difficult in the future... The pattern of changing sex partners therefore seems to damage their ability to bond in a committed relationship... a lifelong and satisfying relationship.[21]

Perhaps the greatest consequence of misusing our sexuality is that our damaged sexuality may never fully live up to the blessing that God desired for us to enjoy. If you have had sexual relationships with many other people, you may enjoy the sexual pleasure but not fully experience the physical/emotional bond that comes with an exclusive relationship. Most people never notice the loss, because they cannot fathom what could have been.

God can give you a clean heart and a new start!

---

[21] Russell Moore, *Sexual Brokenness, and the Hope of the Gospel*, (Leland House Press), Kindle Edition.

> *But I will bring you health*
> *and will heal you of your wounds-*
> *this is the Lord's declaration!*
>
> Jeremiah 30:17

Earlier, we touched on God's procreative design of sexual intercourse as His ongoing act of creation. In Genesis 4, Adam "knew" Eve, his wife, and she conceived and gave birth to Cain." The act of sexual intercourse is not obscured but instead enriched by the word "knew." Some translations of Scripture use the word, "intimate" which is a good translation, but is too often obscured as a modern secret code for sex alone.

God is revealing to humankind the deep relationship that is possible, when in marriage, a man and a woman know each other physically, emotionally, and relationally. There is a tri-dimensional union of the husband and wife becoming one flesh (Genesis 2:24).

In the Song of Solomon 7:10 we read, "I belong to my love and his desire is for me." A man is never more vulnerable or connected to his wife than when they make love. Too many wives misinterpret their husband's passion for them by separating their person from their sexuality: "all he wants is sex." Many men reinforce this by failing to study their wife and engage with her emotionally and verbally. God's design is for sexual intimacy to bond you together and connect you permanently and closely.

Human sexuality is intensely pleasurable for most people, and God intended for it to delight and unite a husband and wife. There are several passages in Scripture that remind us that sexual relationships should be fun and pleasurable; in fact, the Song of Solomon is all about the joy of marital sexuality.

The Song of Solomon has always been confusing to interpreters, and commentators have various biblical interpretations that range from the book being only about God's love for Israel or Christ's love for the church to the book being a collection of love poems. The clearly suggestive and sensuous descriptions in the book celebrate the power of love's intimacy.

Proverbs 5:18-19, "Let your fountain be blessed,
and take pleasure in the wife of your youth.
A loving deer, a graceful doe—
let her breasts always satisfy you;
be lost in her love forever.

This explicit, yet artistic, language seems to eliminate the position that this is only about God's love for Israel or the church. Further, Paul's writings in Ephesians 5 indicate that God does see marriage as a metaphor to his faithful love. Let us be clear, however wonderful the intimacy between a husband and a wife, the ultimate intimacy we will enjoy in Christ will far transcend human sexuality.

One final word, sex brings glory to God when His children enjoy His goodness through His good gifts and give thanks to Him. Yay, God!

1. Why did God establish marriage?
2. How did God intend for marriage to bless humanity?
3. What was God thinking when He created sexual intimacy?
4. How did the fall affect marriage?
5. How did Paul's words in Ephesians 5 help to enable strong marriages in a broken world with two broken people?
6. What do you think of Paul's commandment for wives to submit to their husbands and husbands to love their wives?
7. How does the Bible teach that marriage is a metaphor for the love God has for His people?

THE FAMILY IS ABOUT RELATIONSHIPS

In the cradle of marriage, the family was birthed. Marriage is the foundation of the family. God tells Adam and Eve, "Be fruitful, multiply, fill the earth, and subdue it" (Genesis 1:28). Immediately after the fall, Genesis reports, "The man was intimate with his wife Eve, and she conceived and gave birth to Cain. She said, "I have had a male child with the LORD's help." She also gave birth to his brother, Abel (Genesis 4:1-2).

The physical oneness of marriage led to the birth of children who needed to be nurtured and taught. Like every human being since the fall, their children were raised and taught about life by their parents, in their family. We come into this world bent toward original sin. The operating system, "Rebellion" is loaded automatically. It must be tamed; this is the parent's job.

By Genesis 4, we discover that Adam and Eve's family was in trouble. Cain's failure to follow God's prescription for worship leads to anger, jealousy, and murder. The stage is set for every story of the dysfunctional biblical families to come.

We continue to see the same dysfunction today.

Mountains of research tell us that children reared outside of intact marriages are much more likely than other kids to slip into poverty, become victims of child abuse, fail at school and drop out, use illegal drugs, launch into premature sexual activity, become unwed teen mothers, divorce, commit suicide and experience other signs of mental illness, become physically ill, and commit crimes and go to jail. On average, children reared outside of marriage are less successful in their careers, even after controlling not only for income but also for parental conflict.[22]

Wilcox reports that, "Children who grow up in married, two-parent families have two to three times more positive life outcomes than those who do not."[23] The truth is that healthy societies need healthy families.

Genesis tells many stories about families, including Adam & Eve's, Abraham & Sarah's, Jacob & Rachel's, and Joseph's. The stories are too detailed to describe here, but they are stories as current as this afternoon's soap operas. There is manipulation, lies, lack of faith, competition, jealousy, insecurity, anger, and conflict. There are weak fathers and manipulating mothers. There is the untamed recklessness of an Esau and the deceit of a Jacob. There is pain and heartache everywhere. Such is family life in a fallen world.

---

[22] Linda J. Waite and Maggie Gallagher, *The Case for Marriage: Why Married People Are Happier, Healthier, and Better Off Financially*, (Broadway Books, 2020), Kindle Edition.

[23] W. Bradford Wilcox, *The State of Our Unions: The Surprising Economic Benefits of Marriage*, 2010, 86.

The fifth of the Ten Commandments serves as instruction for the family, "Honor your father and your mother" is critical to the establishment of the new nation, Israel (Exodus 20:12). The Hebrew word for "honor" means to be heavy or weighty. Like rocks laden with gold are heavier than the surrounding rocks, the word means "to be valued." We give our time, attention, and gratitude to people who we honor.

Children learn respect for authority in the home. If they do not learn it at home, they are unlikely to learn it elsewhere. Society's foundation is the home. The Apostle Paul helps us understand how this is done in Ephesians 6:1-4, "don't stir up anger in your children, but bring them up in the training and instruction of the Lord." These two words sound synonymous, but each has its own nuance. "Training" shades toward nurturing to maturity while "instruction" shades toward discipline. Children need to be raised with loving guidance and discipline. Note God's warning against over-discipline that "stirs up anger." The Bible never approves of abusive parenting.

Many are blessed to grow up in a home where this is relatively easy. Our parents loved us and cared for us in ways that become increasingly clear as we age. But many people grow up in homes where their parents were self-centered, angry, abusive, substance controlled, and thus damaged them. Many of these people were hurt children who grew up to hurt others.

Therefore, Moses added the last part of the fifth commandment, "so that you may have a long life in the land that the LORD your God is giving you." A society that passes on to the next generation the good laws of God will prosper. A society that loses this foundation will begin to disintegrate in one generation.

There is little doubt that children who grow up in dysfunctional families begin life with a deficit. Children who grow up with love and discipline have the raw material and character to face life and all of its complexities. American society and its laws used to reinforce the clear teachings of Scripture. Increasingly, they no longer do. So, families face the counter-revolutionary challenge of instilling a biblical love and world view in opposition to almost every voice within the competing culture.

God designed the family to be the backbone of civilization. The Hebrew people placed a high value on the education of their children. God's Word and God's law were to be taught to their children. God laid this foundation in the "Shema" found in Deuteronomy 6. These words were and still are crucial to His chosen people, the Jews. The Shema is central to the blessings recited by religious Jews in both their morning and evening prayers.

> Listen, Israel: The LORD our God, the LORD is one. Love the LORD your God with all your heart, with all your soul, and with all your strength. These words that I am giving you today are to be in your heart. Repeat them to your children. Talk about them when you sit in your house and when you walk along the road, when you lie down and when you get up. Bind them as a sign on your hand and let them be a symbol on your forehead. Write them on the

doorposts of your house and on your city gates.
Deuteronomy 6:4-9

It is no accident that God's people, the Jews, survived 1900 years without a homeland or a nation to call their own. Their identity was grounded by each generation passing on the Word of God to the next generation. The Shema became indispensable to the survival of their faith even during the dark days of the Holocaust.

During the Holocaust, many Jewish children were hidden in the homes of sympathetic Europeans and especially in Catholic orphanages. After the war, it was not always clear which children were of Jewish origin and which were not. In 2019, letters were discovered in Israel's National Library archives that authenticated an old story.

One day in 1946, Rabbi Herzog arrived at a large monastery which was known to have taken in Jewish children sent away by their parents to protect them from the Nazi terror which had ravaged Europe. Now, the time had come for the children to return home.

The Rabbi turned to the Reverend Mother, thanking her for saving the lives of the children and requesting to receive them back to the Jewish People, now that the war was over. The nun was happy to agree, but asked the Rabbi – "How can you know which of the hundreds of children here at the monastery are Jewish?" After all, it had been many months since their parents had sent them there, and many had been mere infants at the time.

Rabbi Herzog assured the Reverend Mother that he would know. He asked to gather all of the children in a large hall, ascended the stage, and cried in a loud voice:

Sh'ma Yisrael Adonai Eloheinu Adonai Eḥad ! (Hear, O Israel: the Lord is our God, the Lord is One) Immediately, dozens of children rushed to the stage, shouting "mama!" and "papa!" as tears filled their eyes. Many were sobbing uncontrollably. Though few of the children remembered much of their early lives, the sound of the *Shema*, the most famous prayer in the Jewish faith, instantly brought back memories of reciting these Hebrew words with their parents before bedtime.[24]

From this we learn that faith is both taught and caught from our parents. Children will remember what you say and what you do. Your children will likely do what you do rather than what you say. Faith is sown into the fabric of our children's lives. Life is the classroom for faith. Scripture is the lifeline of faith.

As a dad, I spent too much time away from my children, but we also had great times together. What I remember best about time with my girls was teaching them through silly stories about my childhood. I called them the "Little Boy Named Leo Stories" because they all began with the same opening line, "Many, many moons ago there was a little boy named Leo..." Many of these stories were just silly memories embellished enough to become fun. Many

---

[24] Shai Ben-Ari, "How 500 Children Were Returned to the Jewish People after the Holocaust, Diaspora," August 27, 2019, https://blog.nli.org.il/en/rabbi_herzog/

of them were memories of my mom and dad. Many of them were stories to teach a moral lesson or a biblical truth. By the time the girls were reaching middle school, I wrote all of the stories down and gave them books for Christmas. They are a family treasure of stories that would have been lost but now continue to remind us of the importance of family.

Little Boy Named Leo Story

Many, many moons ago there was a little boy named Leo who had some interesting things in his drawer. You see, in his Boy Scout troop they had put together survival kits to take on their camping trips. In the little boy named Leo's kit he had a flint and steel for starting fires; he had a knife, and he had a mirror for attempting to attract attention by flashing the light of the sun. He also had some basic food stuffs including some gold foil-wrapped bouillon cubes.

One day, the little boy name Leo's brother, Eric had a nosey friend come over and spend the afternoon. Victor had the audacity to open the little boy named Leo's drawer and start rummaging around in it. When he spotted the foil-wrapped cubes he helped himself, thinking he'd found some candy. You should have seen the look on his gagging face when he bit into that cube. "Yuk! Yuk! Yuk! He hollered as he ran to the bathroom. Boy did he get what he deserved!

Additionally, I'd sing songs from my childhood, songs my dad taught us. Mostly the words were only slightly changed, but the girls have since said that they will never really know the real words to some of these songs. We especially loved singing "We're Going to Kansas City" because we were often driving through KC to see grandparents in Missouri. I personalized it for the two little girls in the backseat of our car:

We're going to Kansas City
Kansas City here I come.
We're going to Kansas City
Kansas City here I come.
I've got some crazy little ladies
In the back seat of my car.

We also read a great deal to our kids. The family favorite was C. S. Lewis' *The Chronicles of Narnia*. Night after night we would read at least one chapter. The girls would beg us to read at least one more.

Kids feel the love of parents when we spend time with them. Reading, drinking imaginary tea, going to the park, taking them to dance, school, sports, drama... etc. Our kids experience our love when we spend time with them.

Years ago, my mom and I were in the car and heard the old seventies song, "Cats in the Cradle." My mom said to me, your dad hated that song because it reminded him of all the times he told you boys he didn't have time to play catch with you. I found that odd, I didn't remember things that way; I remember a dad who loved playing catch with his sons. If we love our kids and they know we love them, they often forget the bad and remember the good.

Parents should understand the various messages we send our children. We teach them that God says, "Don't lie... don't steal" but then we sell a car with major hidden defects at a high price and celebrate our cunning. We demand that our kids control their anger and language but then we blow up frequently at the littlest thing. We drink too much and then tell our children to stay away from alcohol. We claim God is important, but then skip church frequently for less important things.

The Apostle Paul writes in the simplest of terms about this complex and critical interaction within the family.

> Children, obey your parents in the Lord, because this is right. Honor your father and mother, which is the first commandment with a promise, so that it may go well with you and that you may have a long life in the land. Fathers, don't stir up anger in your children, but bring them up in the training and instruction of the Lord. Ephesians 6:1-4

I grew up in a home where the "Texas Belt" reinforced obedience. It was rarely used, but often threatened. Generally, I accepted the verdict that I deserved. My mom and dad were not vindictive, they were full of love and grace, but they knew three boys needed discipline. There were times when I received punishment for things I didn't do. Those were dangerous times because I stewed in the injustice of what had happened. It caused me to doubt the goodness of my parents. I grew to understand that my parents were not mean, though they were sometimes wrong. As a parent myself, I came to understand the complexity of disciplining a child.

Good parenting does not guarantee obedient children. Children are born with their own minds and their own bent. Parents, while hopefully the most powerful influence on a child, are not the only influence affecting the development of a child. In fact, very early in a child's life the influence of parents is challenged by the child's peers. Typically, as the child grows older so does the power of his/her peers. At some point the influence of one's peers overtakes the influence of one's parents. Peers have an overpowering influence when children are young. The desire to fit in and be accepted can overcome even the most fully grounded child. Additionally, injustice can warp children's perspective. A harsh parent can lead to rebellion, Ephesians 6:3. In this fallen world, so much can go wrong.

We all know the old expression, "What goes around comes around." If we do not teach our children to honor and respect us, they will not respect the authorities they meet at school, on the job, in public safety or life in general. Ultimately, they will not honor us in our old age either. The Bible teaches respect for the elderly and the responsibility of children to care for their elders in their old age. I frequently hear people my age teasing each other to treat their children well because their children will ultimately choose their nursing home.

Young people can easily dismiss what they believe to be weak beliefs about life and accept alternative answers that appear to be wiser or fit their lifestyle. Often, they uncritically accept entire systems of beliefs based on the perception of finding something new, fresh and exciting. They buy an alternative world view because it seems to strike some chord within their own personal struggle.

Many of them return to their roots later in life as they come with mature minds to reexamine their beliefs and the beliefs of their parents. Unfortunately, some never reexamine the faith of their childhood and live an unexamined life.

My dad was born in 1936 and grew up in what was then the much smaller city of Houston, Texas. His parent's marriage broke up when his mother met a semi-pro baseball player named Leo Ostenberg.

Leo was an alcoholic. He had played baseball for many minor league teams including the San Francisco Seals and the Sacramento Senators. He was good, batting .304 with 91 home runs in his 877-game career. He got his shot at the majors when he was "discovered" by Babe Ruth. The family story is that he played the preseason with the New York Yankees, but before the first regular season game he got drunk, bought a motorcycle, and did not show up for the game. He was released and returned to the minors where he bounced around from team to team until 1940.

He finished his baseball career as the batting coach for the New York Yankees. My brother once had a copy of the 1941 New York Times sport's page showing my grandfather giving advice to Joe DiMaggio late in his famous hitting streak. The caption said something like, "Ostenberg, giving pitching advice to DiMaggio. It must have been good. DiMaggio hit safely in his 52nd game."

Growing up a child of divorce in the 1940s was hard enough, but my dad's stepdad was a mean drunk. My dad, Robert E. Endel grew up neglected while his parents partied. He stayed as far away as he could when his

105

stepdad was drunk. Each summer he went to be with his grandmother who loved him and taught him a better way. She was the one who introduced my dad to Jesus. It is her legacy that ultimately led our family to follow Jesus.

My dad took three things from his stepfather that ended up providing a foundation for his life—two were negative examples my dad turned into positive foundations for our family. Alcohol and divorce were rejected; sobriety and family were established. He vowed that he would never drink, that seemed easy enough, but he only knew how NOT to do family. He determined in his heart that he would not repeat his family's mistakes.

The one positive thing that he received from his stepfather was his love of baseball. Had he had support at home, he would have likely gone to college and played ball. As it was, his priority was to get away from home and any dependence upon his parents. He did this by enlisting in the Air Force and getting as far away as he possibly could. That is how a Houston boy came to meet a Tonopah, Nevada girl.

My mom grew up in a small mining town in Central Nevada—Tonopah. Tonopah was a boom/bust mining town that was originally founded when silver ore was discovered by Jim Butler. Today, millions of Americans know something of Tonopah because of Area 51 and the Tonopah Test Site. Mom was smart, confident, and relational. My dad, the star athlete, was specially flown, from this remote mining town, to California to play baseball for the Air Force team and was noticed by my mom. He too noticed her! She was loved by her parents and taught good manners. She knew what was socially respectable. In many ways, they were a perfect match. She knew the love of a family and modeled it in the way she wanted to raise her family. My aunt is fond of saying that they grew up in a "Leave it to Beaver"[25] kind of family. Because of my grandparent's influence, so did I.

To one degree or another, we all grow up to be like our families of origin or to be different from our families of origin. Regardless, our families shape us and provide a point of reference for every relationship that follows.

Frequently, I hear friends describe how even now, in their fifties or sixties, when they gather with family they immediately slide back into the familiar roles of their childhood. They might be the respected mayor of their community, but they are still third in authority at home.

The Bible does not gloss over the challenges of family life. Even the most casual glance through the Bible reveals the truth that there are no perfect families. Sin is often most viciously revealed to those who know us best.

We tend to pass on what we know. Adam and Eve led the world into sin. They failed to teach their sons clearly about how to relate to God. Unwilling to be corrected by God, Cain lashes out in anger and kills his brother. He is thus banned and removed from the family.

---

[25] *Leave it to Beaver* was a television series that ran from 1957-1963. It continues to be one of the most idyllic family shows to ever run. Many people do not believe these kinds of families existed. Many of us know they did.

Noah is offered as the only righteous man in a world overwhelmed by wickedness, but after the flood, Noah gets drunk and his daughters devise an incestuous plan to give them children.

Abraham is a man of faith who believes God. He obeys God's call to do the ridiculous, "Go to a place I will show you." So, Abraham packs up all his herds and possessions, and all his family and leaves all he knows going to who knows where—incredible faith. God promises to make a great nation from Abraham who has no son. Abraham believes God, but when threated by someone who he imagines might kill him to take his wife Sarah, he lies and says he is her brother. God must step in to preserve Sarah's dignity. God's seemingly unfulfilled promise leads to Sarah and Abraham's sin as they try to fulfill God's promise in their own way. This sinful act of faithlessness results in so much dissention that we still feel the divide four thousand years later in the Jewish (Isaac), Arab (Ishmael) divide.

David's family was a mess as well. David has many wives yet still commits adultery. His oldest son, Amnon rapes his half-sister, Tamar (2 Samuel 13:1-19). David allows this to go unpunished, so Absalom has him murdered. Absalom then leads a rebellion that nearly ends David's reign.

Scripture notes that parents have a long-term influence on their children.

> I, the LORD your God, am a jealous God, bringing the consequences of the fathers' iniquity on the children to the third and fourth generations of those who hate

me, but showing faithful love to a thousand generations of those who love me and keep my commands. Exodus 20:5-6

Sin gets passed from generation to generation. We do what we saw our parents do. We are influenced by their sin. Rebellious parents teach their children to be rebellious. Godless parents teach their children that God does not exist. Angry parents teach their children to be angry. Drunks teach their children to abuse alcohol. Critical people teach their children to be critical. Hateful parents teach their children to hate. Cheaters teach their children to cheat. Liars teach their children to lie. Unfaithful parents teach their children to be unfaithful. We learn from the people who have the most time to influence our behavior during the formative years of our lives. We tend to follow their example. It's what we know.

God seems to always stack the deck in favor of good. The good our parents pass on to us has even more lasting power. We learn to love and care about people from parents that love people. We learn to be honest and tell the truth from parents who are honest. We learn to control our emotions and think through our challenges by parents who have modeled that for us. We learn to be encouraging and generous by parents who showed us how. We learned to be faithful to others by watching our parents be faithful to each other.

The family becomes the crucible for shaping our character and our thinking. Family programs us for success or failure.

Most of us acknowledge the influence of our parents in our life's journey. As we have noted, many people received little or no help from their parents, some were damaged by their influence. As with the example of my dad, even a bad example can still be a great teaching tool.

I am grateful for the examples I received from my parents. Both my mom and my dad gave my brothers and I everything they had. My dad was my hero. He was an amazing athlete. One of my cousins told me once that, "your dad was a Greek god." He was the spiritual backbone of our family and some of my most vivid memories are of him reading his little New Testament. I remember my parents teaching us ethics, discipleship, and church history in Church Training. I also remember the man who worked full-time while going to school full-time to get a teaching degree. I remember a godly leader who served as a faithful deacon and loved his pastor. I remember the man who kissed me goodbye and good night every night—until he died when I was 36. I remember a kind father who would stand up for what was right and wrong, and fervently believed the Bible.

I am grateful that my mom is still alive. She was, and still is, a thoughtful, intelligent, woman with endless energy and insight who will do whatever needs to be done. I remember her as a woman who would do whatever it took to meet the needs of her family and to raise us to be polite, strong, capable young men. I remember a woman who read books three and a half inches thick. A woman who loves dogs and people. A woman who loves her friends and is always there to support them. A woman who passed on to me the ability to read situations and the emotions of people, and a heart to help them when I can.

I have often said that the greatest Christmas gift I ever received wasn't a present for me. It was a present my dad gave my mom in 1977. I was working at the Base Commissary (a grocery store on a military base)—my first real job--$5-12/day and $15-25 on Saturdays. I had money for the first time in my life.

Four years earlier, the Air Force claimed to have overpaid dad for the three years we were in Alaska—he didn't get paid at all for several months. They never recovered financially. It was during that time that mom and dad had agreed not to give gifts to each other so they could afford to give gifts to us—their three sons. But this year my dad would break his promise: mom hadn't had a coffee pot for years—it was one of those luxuries that she gave up to make ends meet.

That year, every time you turned on the television, Joe DiMaggio was hawking the Mr. Coffee pot. Apparently, at some point my mom had mentioned that she would really like one of those—my dad determined he would get one for her. One night, before Christmas my dad asked me to buy his watch for $20 or $30, I don't really remember the amount anymore. You should know that my dad only had two possessions: his wedding ring and his watch. I told him that I would give him the money, letting him keep the watch, but he wouldn't accept it; he was persistent, so I finally bought his watch; he bought the Mr. Coffee pot.

Over the next several days, I couldn't help but notice the

white strip of skin across his tanned wrist where his watch used to be. I couldn't stand it and I didn't know what to do.

We always celebrated Christmas on Christmas Eve, my dad's birthday. As usual, we went to the Christmas Eve service at First Baptist Church, Knob Noster, Missouri then hurried home for Christmas snacks, the reading of the Christmas story out of Luke's gospel, and then the finale—opening our Christmas presents. We always went slow, opening one present at a time so we could savor each present under the tree. As we finished with the last gift, my dad announced that there was one more and reached behind the tree for a present. He gave it to my mom who protested that they had agreed not to do this—but she opened the present and was delighted. "Where did you get the money?" she asked. He avoided her question.

We sat talking and eating and trying out our new presents when I announced I had one more gift for dad—his birthday present. I pulled it out and passed it to dad who immediately knew what I'd done. He opened it and immediately the whole family knew what had happened—it was his watch. My dad choked up and my mom started crying and finally all of us—three teenage boys and our parents cried like babies.

Looking back forty-three years ago, it wasn't about Christmas presents, coffee pots, or watches. It was about the sacrificial love of my father. His love still flows in me today, and when I hear his watch tick, I think of him and am challenged to be like him today.

Whether our family gave us a positive or a negative example, it is important not to see this as an excuse for our own sinfulness or become self-righteousness. We are not fated to repeat the mistakes of our family; similarly, we are not destined for sainthood. At some point, most of us begin to think for ourselves and make our own choices about life and our behavior. Unfortunately, it is easier to repeat the mistakes we have grown accustomed to than it is take responsibility for who we are and chart a new path. Fortunately, it is usually easier to walk in the steps of godly parents. They have shown us the way family works.

Early in ministry, I was part of a 70th Anniversary celebration for a couple in the church that I pastored. They were good and godly people greatly respected in the community. When the extended family arrived, I observed five generations of people who had followed the path Joe and Ruth Mohler had blazed. It was an unusual group. With few exceptions the room was filled with smiles, laughter, and joy. Generation by generation they had taught the next generation how to love God and love others. God's plan for the family works!

Some individuals have every benefit of a good and godly family but choose their own way. Why would a child look at a good and loving family and decide to choose another way? A thirty-five-year marriage may seem boring and dull on the outside. Young people, in their youth, often value the wrong things. Their choices are based on the pleasure of today, but the long-term impact is hazy. Youthful vision may not take them to the peace and fulfillment of a life well lived.

Many things can draw individuals from the path set by their family. Alcohol and drug abuse destroy millions of lives. The appeal of money, sex, and fame offer what can never be delivered—an intoxicating feeling of success and power. The teenage years are tough and the power of friends, acquaintances, celebrities, and the deep desire within most of us to be accepted and belong draws us to do things for the acceptance and praise of others.

All of these things promise an exciting way to live but the pleasure tingles for a moment and then bites for a lifetime. Even the smallest of decisions here and there can throw you off of life's path without a compass. You grasp the next thing in the path hoping it will bring satisfaction and you feel the high of the moment and then it gives way to an emptiness that must be filled with the next thrill. After a while you feel like rats being led through a meaningless exercise of pleasure and pain that satisfies something in us for a second but then leaves us empty and hungry for something more, something better. We are insatiable; we can never be satisfied.

Unfortunately, like King Solomon of the Bible, it takes us a lifetime to discover that things and experiences never do satisfy. It is only in relationships that we find deep and satisfying joy... especially in a relationship with God.

For those who grew up in difficult families, without good examples, God graciously reaches out to us and gives us off ramps to show us that we can choose another way. God gives us friends and neighbors that live God's way. Their lives stand out to us as a testimony to the goodness of following God. Perhaps someone tries to explain the gospel to you. Perhaps someone invites you to church or a small group. Perhaps a friend shares their faith with you and prays for you during a difficult time. You can break free.

In these days of mobility, family is often less involved in our lives. Thanksgivings and Christmas's come and go as we interact with each other for a few hours or days and then retreat to our individual lives. Often, it is the health emergency or the death of a parent that draw us back together and forces us to deal with each other again.

For those who grew up in angry or abusive homes, you may never see repentance and restoration. Some people are so damaged that it will take a miracle for them to change. Some are already dead and gone. My step grandfather seemed unreachable, but he was ultimately changed by the gospel.

In the late 1950's, sometime after my dad left home, my grandfather was sitting at a bar doing what he had always done, but something happened. He began to think about all he had lost in his life because of his alcoholism. He had a single silver dollar in left in his pocket. He could buy a couple more beers or he could keep it as a reminder of the day he decided not to drink again. I have that silver dollar today. It is completely smooth, even the serrated edges of the coin are gone. I remember, long before I knew the significance, watching my grandfather holding the coin, rubbing the coin as he watched sports on his big color TV.

Around twenty years later, the man who was party to an affair, a broken marriage, and the angry and uncaring treatment of his stepson came face to face with his need for a Savior and repented of his sins receiving new life in Jesus Christ.

I now remember him sitting at the kitchen table of their little house reading the Bible and praying, early in the morning. I remember him talking about the Lord. Who could have ever thought this was possible? He was now in relationship with God and his family.

Questions for Discussion

1. How has your family of origin shaped you to be the person you are today?
2. In what ways has their influence been good on you?
3. In what ways has their influence led you into brokenness and sin?
4. What family stories have been preserved that point to sin or pain, and what family stories have provided positive examples of courage and faith?
5. How seriously have you taken the biblical challenge to teach your children?
6. Are you passing on your faith to the next generation?
7. Are their broken family relationships that you could initiate healing?
8. Do you continue to pray for those who have walked away from a biblical understanding of life and accountability to God?

FRIENDSHIP IS ABOUT RELATIONSHIPS

According to my Facebook page I have over two-thousand friends! Yeah, right! What does it mean to be a friend? I looked up "friendship" in online dictionaries only to find definitions that were not helpful. In the Britannica Dictionary I found the most helpful definition: a state of enduring affection, esteem, intimacy, and trust between two people.[26]

The Mayo Clinic website notes that "friendship enriches your life and improves your health."[27] Dana Sparks writes of the benefits of friendship:

- Increase your sense of belonging and purpose
- Boost your happiness and reduce your stress
- Improve your self-confidence and self-worth
- Help you cope with traumas, such as divorce, serious illness, job loss or the death of a loved one

---

[26] Britannica, "Friendship",
https://www.britannica.com/topic/friendship
[27] Dana Sparks, "Mayo Mindfulness: Friendships Enrich Your Life and Improve Your Health", September 4, 2019.

- Encourage you to change or avoid unhealthy lifestyle habits, such as excessive drinking or lack of exercise[28]

Friendship doesn't come cheap. A 2018 study done by researcher, Jeffrey Hall, talks about the personal hours of interaction needed to develop friendships. Clearly, time limits the number of friends one person can develop or maintain. Hall notes the time investment necessary to develop friendships:

- 40-60 hours to form a casual friendship
- 80-100 hours to become a friend
- 200+ hours to become a good friend[29]

According to anthropologist Robin Dunbar we have the mental capacity to handle no more than approximately 150 friendships. Dunbar says most people have five intimate friends, fifteen close friends, fifty good friends, around 150 casual friends, 500 acquaintances, 1500 people you can recognize.[30] Though the actual numbers vary from person to person the general principles are accurate. You cannot have 2000 close friends!

---

[28] Ibid.
[29] Jeffrey A. Hall, Journal of Social and Personal Relationships, "How Many Hours Does It Take to Make a Friend," March 15, 2018.
[30]Christine Ro, "Dunbar's number: Why we can only maintain 150 relationships", BBC Future, October 9, 2019.
https://www.bbc.com/future/article/20191001-dunbars-number-why-we-can-only-maintain-150-relationships

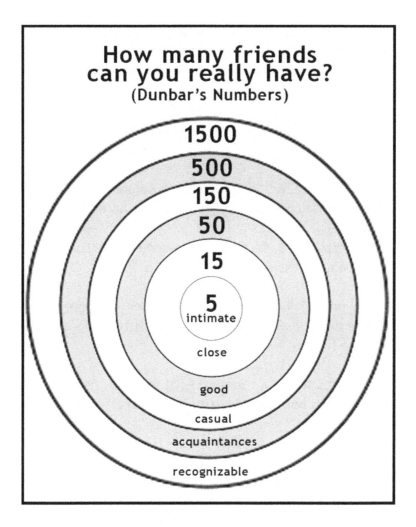

How many friends can you really have?
(Dunbar's Numbers)

1500
500
150
50
15
5
intimate

close

good

casual

acquaintances

recognizable

Friendships can be positive or negative. Most of us think of peer pressure in a negative sense, but peer pressure can be a positive force as well. We can be influenced by our friends toward misery or we can be influenced by our friends to be happy. The best friendships bring out the best in each other.

The book of Proverbs gives amazing insight regarding friendship. Very little needs to be added regarding one's selection of friends and the influence of friendship.

Proverbs 12:26, "The righteous choose their friends carefully, but the way of the wicked leads them astray."

Proverbs 13:20, "Walk with the wise and become wise, for a companion of fools suffers harm."

Proverbs 16:28, "A perverse person stirs up conflict, and a gossip separates close friends."

Proverbs 17:9, "Whoever would foster love covers an offense, but whoever repeats the matter separates close friends."

Proverbs 17:17, A friend loves at all times, and a brother is born for adversity."

Proverbs 22:24-25, "Don't make friends with an angry person, and don't be a companion of a hot-tempered one, or you will learn his ways and entangle yourself in a snare."

Proverbs 18:24, "One who has unreliable friends soon comes to ruin, but there is a friend who sticks closer than a brother."

Proverbs 27:5-6, Better is open rebuke than hidden love. Wounds from a friend can be trusted, but an enemy multiplies kisses."

Proverbs 27:9-10, "the sweetness of a friend is better than self-counsel. Don't abandon your friend or your father's friend..."

Proverbs 27:17, As iron sharpens iron, so one person sharpens another."

The Old Testament wisdom literature extends into the book of Ecclesiastes with the wise man examining the purpose of life, and specifically here, friendship:

Two are better than one because they have a good reward for their efforts. For if either falls, his companion can lift him up; but pity the one who falls without another to lift him up. Also, if two lie down together, they can keep warm; but how can one person alone keep warm? And if someone overpowers one person, two can resist him. A cord of three strands is not easily broken. (Ecclesiastes 4:9-10)

In friendship, there is a synergy of effort when two people work together. 1 + 1 no longer equals two, but instead three. We get a "good reward" for our efforts together. We can accomplish more together than we can alone.

Second, friends can support each other in times of difficulty, "if either falls, his companion can lift him up; but pity the one who falls without another to lift him up." We "get by with a little help from our friends."

Third, friends find mutually beneficial physical and emotional support, "if two lie down together, they can keep warm; but how can one person alone keep warm?"

This metaphor has its literal application in travelers sharing body heat when sleeping in the cold. But theologian Duane Garret says this metaphor is also about "emotional comfort against the coldness of the world." [31]

Finally, friends find strength for facing life and working together, "And if someone overpowers one person, two can resist him. A cord of three strands is not easily broken." When I was in elementary school outside of Fairbanks, Alaska we played King of the Mountain on the snow heaps beside the school parking lot. My brother Eric was only two years younger than me and we found that if the two of us could get to the top of the mountain and stand back-to-back there wasn't anyone who could throw us off.

Friendship is powerful! But Paul, and some of the Proverbs, also remind us of the negative influence of poorly chosen friends, "Do not be deceived: 'Bad company corrupts good morals'" (1 Corinthians 15:33).

I find it amazing that Jesus, the Son of God, calls us his friends, but He does:

> "No one has greater love than this: to lay down his life for his friends. You are my friends if you do what I command you. I do not call you servants anymore, because a servant doesn't know what his master is doing. I have called you friends, because I have made

---

[31] Duane A. Garrett, *The New American Commentary: Proverbs, Ecclesiastes, Song of Songs,* (Nashville, Broadman & Holman, 1993), Kindle Edition.

known to you everything I have heard from my Father. John 15:13-15

"Friends are friends forever" sang Michael W. Smith, but this is rarely true. Most of us will have many friends over the course of our lifetime. We will enrich each other's lives for a time and even play critical roles in our future development, but like in the theater, people enter and exit never to be seen again. Recently, I paused and looked at one of our wedding pictures from thirty-five years ago. The people in that picture were my closest friends. Though we are still "Facebook friends" we rarely speak to or see each other. We move and change jobs. We meet new people. Our family develops and so does theirs. The daily routines that once brought us together are disrupted and we, like they, have changed. Life has its way of causing ongoing social upheaval. It's not likely that your seventeen-year-old BFF (Best Friend Forever) will remain your BFF. But remember this, these friends enriched and continue to influence your life.

My high school music teacher, Michael Quimby, had a tremendous influence on me. It is in part his story that began this book. Because of the accident and the excellence of his pipe organ creativity and skills, our lives were intertwined for five to six years. We became very good friends. Michael's organizational skills and communication skills still influence me today. He helped sharpen my speaking skills and our conversations led to spiritual depth and to an expansion of my understandings of other denominational churches. He helped develop me into a leader. Our lives are busy, and we rarely connect today, but his influence on me continues. He is still my friend.

Questions for Discussion

1. What makes a friend a friend?
2. Who are your closest friends?
3. Who are active friends in your second-tier friendship circle?
4. Have you come to accept that even great friends come and go during differing seasons of life?
5. Among your friends, which are the most helpful, encouraging and fulfilling to you spiritually?
6. Do you have friends that are primarily a negative influence on you?
7. Are you investing time in friendships that do not fulfill the wisdom of the Proverbs?
8. What can you do to be a better friend?

EDUCATION IS ABOUT RELATIONSHIPS

The influence of teachers, coaches, bosses, and mentors can hardly be overestimated. Classroom teachers spend around 1000 hours per year influencing a child. These relationships shape us for our future relationships. They teach us about life.

Most kid's coaches never took a class on coaching, and most of them think they know more about the sport than they actually do. These coaches simply mimic their childhood coaches—good and bad. Their character shapes their influence.

My first year of elementary school tackle football my brother Eric and I were put on the Chargers football team. Coach Mikula was a surly profane man who couldn't speak a sentence without at least some coarse language. As a fifth grader I was shocked. We didn't talk like that at home, and I wanted to quit. Fortunately, I had a godly dad. When I told him about our coach, he gave Eric and I a "man talk" that affirmed our reaction at this man's language, but he told us we had better learn to live with such people. Dad told us we could quit if we wanted to, but if we did, we couldn't change our minds and go back. Clearly, he thought it best for us to persevere. We did.

I am grateful for the teachers who influenced me. Never underestimate the power of your spoken words. Fifty years later, I still remember my sixth-grade teacher telling me I was going to do great things in my life, "Someday, I'll read about you in the national news." So far, she hasn't, but her encouragement still stirs me today.

When I was in high school, in Knob Noster, Missouri, I had amazing teachers. Though this school graduates less than 100 students per year, it continues to be ranked in the top ten schools in the state of Missouri. Ask anyone about the spiritual and academic influence of Mrs. Delores Craig. She demanded excellence from us and got it even from students most people believed to be incorrigible. Mrs. Craig was a master teacher. She died earlier this year and students posted memories of her teaching and her influence. I will never forget her pride the year three of us represented Knob Noster in the model United Nations competition. At the meeting, we found out we were to play the role of Saudi Arabia. Because she had taught us well, we ran the U.N. meeting. She never said a word, she just beamed with pride. Her confidence in us empowered us. If a winning team could have been announced, we knew it would have been us. She had made us ready for world affairs.

Dr. Wilbur Thielbar was an active member of the church I attended in college and was a key professor of finance at the local university. Wilbur loved God and operated with distinction in the university context. He both served as an example and an inspiration for my faith and ministry. God used him to point me to business and finance before calling me into ministry. Wilbur mentored and advocated for me. Years later I would be able to see God's hand on Thielbar's guidance when I came to be the operations director for the Minnesota-Wisconsin Baptist Foundation.

In seminary, several professors expanded my understanding of life and theology. T. B. Maston had long ago retired from teaching, but I read his books, and was so inspired that my wife made a contact with Dr. Maston that led me into a close personal friendship with a man who had once fought racism on a national stage. I spent time in his home helping he and his wife with the daily care of their physically and mentally challenged son, Tom Mac. Many a morning began at their breakfast table hearing the morning devotional before I went to class or work. His influence still guides me to this day.

A Special Word to Teachers

If you're like most teachers, you are nearly always worn to a frazzle and beat down by the daily battles with students and their parents. You're underpaid and your work is never done. It's very easy to let the frustration and anger you experience with a few kids and parents overwrite the positive influence you have on the majority.

There are no easy solutions to tame the beast in an eighth grader. Remember that her brain isn't even yet fully developed. She isn't logical. She doesn't follow through. Her dog may have eaten her homework! She doesn't believe she'll ever use algebra, and maybe she won't. You're trying to help kids develop a knowledge base for a life they can't even yet imagine.

At the end of the day they might not learn everything that we think they should learn, but we will fight for them to become more than they can see. Encourage them and push them. At the end of the year they will move on and likely forget much of what you tried to teach them. But if you cared for them, if you loved them, if you did your best to draw out of them their best, you have made a difference. In the end, even education is all about relationships.

What you're doing is worth it. Don't give up! These kids need you! Yes, you would make more money administrating the sale of widgets. Yes, it would be nice to come home at night and not grade papers. Yes, you wouldn't have nasty emails to answer from angry parents whose behavior explains why their children are difficult in the classroom.

What you are doing is worth it. You are making a difference, even when you think you're not. Remember Mrs. Craig I mentioned earlier? Some of the tributes I read from fellow students shocked me. They were from kids I remember trying to sleep through class (though she never allowed that); they were from kids who rarely made a knowledgeable comment in our discussions; they were from kids that I was certain didn't care. But their comments told a different story. They remembered a teacher who didn't so much fight against them but fought for them. They remembered a teacher who cared.

Teachers, thank you for all you do!

Questions for Discussion

1. Why is teaching about relationships?
2. What kind of influence does a classroom teacher have on his/her pupils?
3. What kind of influence does a coach have on her athletes?
4. Who are the teachers and coaches that influenced you? What did they teach you?

LEADERSHIP IS ABOUT RELATIONSHIPS

Jesus said, "Follow me" and they did! Today around two billion people claim to be following Jesus. Leadership is all about relationships.

Business leadership experts, Blanchard and Hodges write, "When all the facts are fairly considered, we may safely say that Jesus Christ is the most effective leader the world has ever known."[32] Though many might deny the divinity of Jesus, few can deny the power of His words and teaching. Jesus changed the world.

Recently, a student challenged one of my colleagues by saying that today's fascination with leadership is not biblical because the word does not occur in the Bible. Wow! First, it does; secondly, the Bible is full of leaders and their stories. Dozens of biblical words are used to define leadership.

Robert Clinton offers the classic Christian definition of a leader:

---

[32] Ken Blanchard, Phil Hodges, Bob Briner, Ray Pritchard, *More Leadership Lessons of Jesus,* (Nashville: Broadman and Holman Publishers, 1998), 1.

A leader is a person (1) with God-given capacity and (2) with God-given responsibility to influence (3) a specific group of God's people (4) toward God's purposes for the group.[33]

Clinton's definition focuses on the relational dimension of leadership. Leadership is about relationships!

- The leader is in relationship with God for both leadership capacity and responsibility.
- The leader is in relationship with a specific group of people.
- The leader moves that group of people on to God's agenda.

Secular leadership experts Kouzes and Posner write, "Leadership is a relationship. Leadership is a relationship between those who aspire to lead and those who choose to follow."[34]

Kouzes and Posner offer five "Practices of Exemplary Leadership" that could have been based on principles drawn from Jesus.

- Model the way
- Inspire a shared vision
- Challenge the process
- Enable Others to act
- Encourage the heart[35]

Jesus consistently modeled his servant leadership among his disciples. He taught them and served them to show

---

[33] J. Robert Clinton, *The Making of a Leader*, (Colorado Springs: NavPress, 1988), 197.
[34] James Kouzes and Barry Z. Posner, *The Leadership Challenge*, (San Francisco: Jossey-Bass, 3rd ed, 2002), 20.
[35] Kouzes and Posner, 13.

them what godly leadership looks like. Though deserving to be served, Jesus modeled menial tasks like washing his disciple's feet. He showed them how leaders serve those they lead. Jesus said, "If anyone wants to be first, he must be last and servant of all" (Mark 9:35). Jesus showed us that leaders must serve those who follow them.

Jesus inspired his disciples with a vision greater than they could possibly understand and prepared them for their future leadership role. Leaders seek to lead God's people to a vision that is greater than anything they could possibly imagine. Jesus' vision was of changed hearts, forgiveness, redemption, and the healing of man's alienation with God.

Jesus challenged the status quo by revealing God's fulfillment of the old law. He showed that the past revealed the future, but that God's future for them would require change and sacrifice.

Jesus enabled His disciples to act. We see examples of Jesus teaching his disciples about the Kingdom of God and then sending them out to share redemption with the people of Israel. When they returned, he debriefed them on what had occurred and helped them understand the next steps of development necessary for them to lead. This on-the-job training helped to make these men super-natural leaders. They turned the world upside down to fulfill Jesus' vision, the Great Commission.

Jesus encouraged their hearts. Jesus constantly reminded His disciples that He would be with them always. He prepared them for his absence by helping them understand that His Spirit would come and empower them to fulfill the vision.

A leader can't lead well until he/she can understand their own leadership tendencies and the tendencies of those who they work with. Remember, leadership is about relationships. I have frequently used the DISC profile to help church leadership teams and our convention staff understand their roles within our respective teams. The DISC profile shows the basic personalities of each individual team member and how they fit into a working team. One of the primary characteristics of DISC is a person's tendencies for relationship. Most people primarily relate to people and work out of one of these four quadrants.

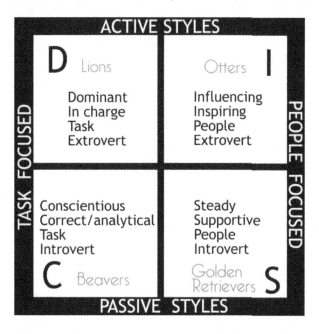

D-Dominance (directive, task orientated leadership) the ferocious lions. D-leaders want to be in charge; they will get the job done even if it kills those they lead. It's all about the task.

I-Influence (engaging, people orientated leadership) the playful otters. I-leaders love people and want to influence others; they value the relationships with people more than the task at hand.

S-Steadiness (reflective, supportive, people-oriented leadership) the Golden Retrievers. S-leaders love people and make good collaborators who hold the group together and serve the good of the group.

> *Christian leadership overcomes the tension between accomplishing the task and caring about people by making the people the task.*

C-Conscientiousness (reflective, task-oriented leadership) the precise beavers. C-leaders are all about doing the job right. They are focused on the details and less interested in relationships.

All these personality types can be leaders, if they understand the tendencies within their personalities. Often the challenge is the tension between getting the job done or caring for the people. Blanchard writes about how Jesus resisted the "tyranny of the or" and "modeled a 'both/and' point of view."[36] I summarize it this way, Jesus solved this dichotomy by "making the people the task."

Certainly, if your job is making widgets at the factory, you can't just focus on the people—it's your job to make widgets, but the Kingdom of God isn't about the things of this world, the Kingdom of God is about people. Christian leadership must always ultimately be about people.

---

[36] Blanchard and Hodges, 111.

134

Years ago, our church built a gymnasium, then a sanctuary, renovated the old building, and started to plan for an office complex. We had to work hard to remember that our primary task was reaching people not building buildings. You can be consumed with hammers and nails, raising money, coordinating volunteers and professional construction people. Too easily you can be so focused on the task that you forget your real task is reaching people. Building the church is far more important than building a church building.

Warner and Wilder write about the importance of relational skills in leadership:

> ...according to a ton of research, performance success in leadership is one-third IQ and two-thirds EQ. Or to put it another way, emotional intelligence counts for twice as much as IQ and technical skills combined to be successful in leading others.[37]

Did you get that? Leadership is only one-third about technical skills and technique; it is two-thirds about relational skills. Leadership is about relationships.

Questions for Discussion:

1. Why would Jesus be called the greatest leader who has ever lived?
2. Why is leadership all about relationships?
3. What kind of a leader are you?
4. Why is leadership more about EQ than IQ?

---

[37] Marcus Warner and Jim Wilder, *Rare Leadership: 4 Uncommon Habits for Increasing Trust, Joy, and Engagement in the People You Lead,* (Chicago: Moody Publishers, Kindle Edition).

THE BIBLE IS ABOUT RELATIONSHIPS

God has loved us through the wisdom of His Word, the Bible. In the Bible God reveals Himself, His purpose, and His ways. He presents us example after example, teaching after teaching of how His followers have lived in this broken world. These are not just laws, but stories and examples of people just like us. God shares these things to help us understand the journey and live through life in the best of all possible ways.

I have found the following diagram to be of help in understanding the full storyline of the Bible. From beginning to end, God is creating and restoring us into perfect relationship with Himself. The Bible is all about relationships!

The Bible chronicles the story of mankind from the mind of God, through creation, the fall, the law, the birth, death, and resurrection of Jesus, to the new heaven and the new earth. Mankind was birthed out of the eternal conversation within the Trinity, we were separated from God by sin, and God has taken the initiative to reunite us with Himself through Jesus Christ. Jesus, alone, stands as

136

the link between God and man; He alone can restore our relationship with God and with each other.

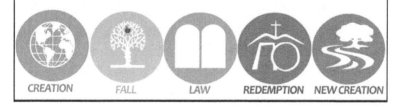

The Bible is all about Relationships

CREATION · FALL · LAW · REDEMPTION · NEW CREATION

I have had the privilege of taking over 200 people on trips to the Holy Land. Year after year new discoveries confirm the accuracy and historicity of the biblical documents. For generations, biblical skeptics denied that Pontius Pilate ever ruled over Israel until the Pilate Stone was discovered at the archaeological site of Caesarea Maritima in 1961. Archaeologist Dr. William F. Albright has written, "There can be no doubt that archaeology has confirmed the substantial historicity of the Old Testament tradition."

Some observations about the Bible:

1. The Bible was written over the course of more than one thousand years by approximately 40 different authors
2. The oldest Scripture fragment of the Bible preserves the modern reading of Numbers 6, the Priestly Blessing, and dates to 586 BC.
3. Bible texts written approximately seven centuries before the time of Christ, before crucifixion was invented, prophesy the details of the crucifixion (Isaiah 53 and Psalm 22).
4. The details of the Old Testament preach Jesus and are fulfilled in Jesus Christ.
5. We have over 5800 ancient Greek manuscripts of the New Testament plus copies in other languages that affirm the accuracy of our modern Bibles.[38]
6. There is an integrated theme and progression from the beginning to the end of the Bible: from Genesis to Revelation.
7. Reading the Bible is dangerous; it will change your life.

Rosaria Butterfield was a professor of English and Women's studies at Syracuse University in the 1990s. She was working on a project to expose the religious right from a lesbian feminist point of view. She believed the Bible was "threatening, dangerous, and irrational."[39]

---

[38] Bryan Windle, Bible Archaeology Report: "The Earliest New Testament Manuscripts", https://biblearchaeologyreport.com/2019/02/15/the-earliest-new-testament-manuscripts/

[39] Rosaria Butterfield, Ligonier Ministries: "An Unlikely Convert: An Interview with Rosaria Butterfield, April 1, 2015.

Through a turn of events she began to ravenously read through the Bible and God brought her to Himself. A friend observed, "This Bible reading is changing you, Rosaria."[40] Yes, reading the Bible is likely to change you. God will reveal Himself to you. "Draw near to God and He will draw near to you" (James 4:8).

THE LAW IS ABOUT LIVING
WITH BROKEN RELATIONSHIPS

After the fall, God loved us by giving us the law. Man cannot live without law. James Madison wrote, "If men were angels, no government would be necessary."[41] In the United States Constitution we find the necessity of law for a free society:

> We the People of the United States, in Order to form a more perfect Union, establish Justice, insure domestic Tranquility, provide for the common defense, promote the general Welfare, and secure the Blessings of Liberty to ourselves and our Posterity, do ordain and establish this Constitution for the United States of America.

Even in the Garden of Eden there was one law. When that law was broken, broken relationships shattered humanity. Human sinfulness exposes our selfishness and propensity toward abusing each other.

---

[40] Rosaria Champagne Butterfield, Christianity Today: "My Train Wreck Conversion", February 7, 2013.
[41] James Madison, The Federalist Paper, No. 51, 1788.

God called a nation, who was not yet a nation, to Himself in the book of Exodus. He gave them the law through which they could build a society. God's laws were not arbitrary. They cannot be improved. They are based upon the character of what is true. They are based upon His perfect character. It is wrong to lie because God is truth. It is wrong to steal because God knows what you need and provides it. It is wrong to commit adultery because marriage is a picture of God's faithfulness. It is wrong to murder because God desires to give us abundant life that can come only from Him.

The law is a series of truth statements revealing the moral mathematics of the universe. As the world operates by physical laws, so does the moral law reveal the reality of God and by extension, the morality woven into God's creation.

God loves us by revealing to us the moral law of the universe. If we live according to His law, we minimize the effects of the fall. He does not want us to needlessly suffer. He wants to guide us to live in the safest and most fulfilling way. Life in this broken, chaotic world is hard enough, we do not need to make it worse by behavior that brings suffering and devastating consequences.

The Lord of the Flies is William Golding's story of a group of English boys shipwrecked on an island and their ensuing struggle to build a society based on accepted rules. In the story, the boys descend into darkness as they try to govern themselves. Strong personalities emerge and a power struggle leads to total breakdown of order and eventually to murder.

Modern societies are faced with a critical problem. If there is no god, who defines what is right and wrong? Who determines the laws by which a society peaceably survives? Does the majority decide what is right and wrong? Does power then ultimately determine whose rules will reign? If there is no God, all is opinion and the power to impose it.

History records scores of dictators who set up their own systems of law to control and brutalize people for their own agendas. How easily we forget the lessons of atheistic regimes and the abuse of law. Mao, Hitler, Stalin, Pol Pot, Kim Il-sung, Idi Amin, and scores of others testify to the brutality of power and law held in the hands of men.

When God delivered his people from Egypt to establish them as a new nation, He knew they would not survive without the gift of law. In the middle of the wilderness, from Mount Sinai, God gave His people exactly what they needed to guide them into right relationship with Himself and with each other. With God's plan in place they would be able to hold together a society based on the revelation of God.

The law of God is part of God's plan to mend a broken world. We are broken people trying to live in community with other broken people. Our human sinfulness exposes our selfishness and propensity toward manipulating others for our benefit. God has a plan to save us from our fallen condition, but in the meantime, we need rules to guide our interactions with others. Only God in His infinite wisdom can lead us through the chaos of our broken thinking. Only He has the wisdom to show us the rules we need to live by in our broken condition.

Here are the Ten Commandments (Exodus 20:3-17):
1. You shall have no other gods before me.
2. You shall not make for yourself any graven image.
3. You shall not take the name of the LORD your God in vain.
4. Remember the sabbath day to keep it holy.
5. Honor your father and your mother.
6. You shall not murder.
7. You shall not commit adultery.
8. You shall not steal.
9. You shall not lie.
10. You shall not covet.

The first four of the Ten Commandments speak to our relationship with God. The next six deal with our relationship with one another.

The ancient world was primarily polytheistic; people believed in many gods. In this world of moral chaos, differing gods called for differing religious practices but few defined right and wrong, only what they required of their worshipers.

The Creator God of Judaism revealed Himself to humanity. As He revealed Himself, He revealed His moral character and thus His moral law. He was more than a figure head to be worshiped, He is the very essence of creation's design and mankind's moral being. Other "gods" are no gods at all. They are fabrications of Satan and our own fallen imaginations; their supposed power and purpose are impotent and empty. Yahweh, the God of the Hebrew people is the One God who holds all created order together. He alone is God.

The Ten Commandments are based upon the preeminence of God and his moral character. Right is right and wrong is wrong, not just because God declared it to be. Right is right because of who God is. The commandments are not arbitrary or pragmatic. The commandments reveal and proclaim the very nature of a good God.

Yale Law School professor, Arthur Leff wrote in 1979:

> Unless there is a God who is himself Goodness and Justice, there can be no ultimate moral basis for the law. For if there is no God, nothing can take his place. No human standard—no person, no group of people, no document—is immune to challenge.[42]

Murder is wrong because God is the giver of life. Adultery is wrong because God is faithful and true. We are not to steal because God knows what we need and is our provider. We are not to lie, because God is the truth. We are not to covet because God, in His generosity, gives us what we need.

THE CROSS IS ABOUT RESTORING RELATIONSHIPS

My father-in-law was a math teacher; my wife is a math teacher; my oldest daughter is a math teacher.

---

[42] Charles Colson and Nancy Pearcey, *How Now Shall We live?* (Tyndale House Publishers, 1999), 408.

Accordingly, one of my favorite stories is about the little boy who was having a terrible time with math. His parents decided, though they were not religious, to enroll him in a catholic school where they had heard the math teacher was excellent. Mom and dad were shocked when on the first day their son walked straight in the door and started to work on his math homework. This had never happened before. After a few days, the parents asked their son about what was going on. The boy answered, "When I walked in that auditorium and saw the guy nailed to the plus sign, I knew these people were serious about math!"

Of course, Catholics are not that serious about math, but they are serious about the cross. Too many Christians barely understand what happened on the cross. We wear crosses around our necks and place them at the front of our worship centers. Most people know that Jesus died on a cross. Fewer understand why. Very few can begin to explain its significance.

The cross of Jesus Christ is the central point of all human history. The Old Testament predicts the cross in detail through passages like Psalm 22 and Isaiah 53. At the cross, relationship comes into focus in a deeply profound way. Within the Trinity, God the Father is at work satisfying His perfect holiness and His love. Christ is reconciling us to God through His sacrificial atoning death. The Holy Spirit is sustaining the Son.[43] (2

---

[43] John Piper, Desiring God, "Where Was the Holy Spirit on Good Friday? Episode 1331, April 127, 2019. https://www.desiringgod.org/interviews/where-was-the-holy-spirit-on-good-friday

Corinthians 5:18-21). We are being reconciled to each other; Christ has broken down the dividing wall of hostility and brought us peace (Ephesians 2:15) through the power of His Spirit (Ephesians 2:18). At the cross God shows His unity and Christ brings us into relationship with God and each other. This is the ultimate reconciliation.

The Trinity is never in conflict. The Father, the Son, and the Holy Spirit are in perfect harmony. They are in perfect interactive relationship. Jesus' incarnation and today's work of the Holy Spirit illustrate for us what it means for God to act in perfect unity within three personalities.

In John 17 we see Jesus talking with His Father about, "completing the work you gave me to do" (John 17:4). As He prays for His disciples, He asks the Father, "protect them by your name that you have given me, so that they may be one as we are one" (John 17:11). Jesus is claiming the relational oneness that He has with the Father and asking that God allow us to be brought into that oneness as well. In other words, God wants to take us from our broken state, alienated from God and make us one with Him in Christ. He wants to reconcile us to Himself.

Further, look at Jesus' words in verse 22, "I have given them the glory you have given me, so that they may be one as we are one." Jesus wants us to be reconciled to each other.

What makes this possible is the cross of Jesus Christ. This prayer is offered hours before the crucifixion. Jesus is in complete unity with the plan of His Father. His desire is to heal our broken relationship with God through the cross. When He pays the debt we owe to God, He makes it possible for us to have the same kind of unity in the relationships we have with others.

The cross is about the character of the God who is just and holy, but also full of love and grace. John 1:14 describes Jesus in just this way, "We observed his glory, the glory as the one and only Son from the Father, full of grace and truth."

The cross is about justice. God is holy and we have wronged Him with our sin. In His perfection, He cannot allow sin in His presence. Thus, we have an impossible problem. We have wronged a Holy God and have no way to heal this wrong. There is nothing we can do.

Fortunately for us, God is also love. He is full of grace. He desires relationship with us—not to complete Himself, for He is already in perfect relationship within the Trinity, but because He created us to be His and display

His glory. How deep is the glory of God? Deep enough to find a way to redeem His rebellious creatures.

How does He do this? God the Son takes on human flesh and lives among us. He lives a perfect, sinless life. He takes your place and my place at the cross. We owe a debt to sin that we cannot pay. God pays the debt on our sin that He did not owe. His love leads Jesus to pay for our rebellion. By faith, we who receive what Jesus has done for us will receive the forgiveness that Jesus offers us.

> *How deep is the glory of God?*
> *Deep enough to find a way*
> *to redeem His rebellious creatures!*

At the cross, Jesus heals our broken relationship with God and makes it possible for us to live at peace with each other. The cross is all about relationships.

THE RESURRECTION
IS ABOUT RESTORING RELATIONSHIPS

The Resurrection is all about relationships—eternal relationships.

On Mother's Day, Becky Amert entered victoriously into the presence of our Lord. Her faith never wavered even when she came to grip with the reality that the Lord was not going to heal her of cancer.

I had just preached the early service at Emmanuel and was standing at the back door when I heard of Becky's death. I rather quickly greeted people and then went over to the Amert's home to pray with Tim and the rest of the family. I do not remember much of our conversation that morning, but I will never forget Tim's words to me, "Pastor, are you preaching good news this morning?" I do not remember what I said, but my mind started racing... they were going to be in church in an hour! Lord, what do you want me to say? I can't preach the same sermon I did at 8:30.

By the time I got to my car I was thinking about the hope of the resurrection... running through a mental index of the New Testament texts that spoke of death and the resurrection. By the time I had made the two-minute trip to Emmanuel, God hit me with a thought. I scrambled to the back of the sanctuary and shuffled through the sermon PowerPoints stored on my computer. There it was. I had written two sermons the week before Easter. By midweek, I had finished one sermon which I felt strongly about. But by Thursday or Friday I just did not feel like that was what I was supposed to preach. So, I set that sermon aside, a little puzzled, but prayed about a new direction and ended up preaching out of 1 Corinthians 15 instead. Now, on Mother's Day, two months later, I quickly glanced through the original Easter sermon while fighting back the tears of realization. God knew when Becky would go home. Weeks before He had laid the plans and the message in place that would minister to a hurting family and a grieving church. The extra sermon on the resurrection was for this moment—out of John 11.

Lazarus had died and Jesus said to Martha:

> "Your brother will rise again," Jesus told her. Martha said to him, "I know that he will rise again in the resurrection at the last day." Jesus said to her, "I am the resurrection and the life. The one who believes in me, even if he dies, will live. Everyone who lives and believes in me will never die."
> John 11:25-26

When you stand in the hospital after the machines have been turned off, when you stand at the graveside of your most precious person in the world, NOTHING! NOTHING! NOTHING! matters more than the resurrection. Jesus said, "Because I live you also shall live" (Jn 14:19). Paul's words have resounded at millions of funerals. "Thanks be to God! He gives us the victory through our Lord Jesus Christ" (1 Corinthians 15:57).

Years later I found comfort again in Paul's words. My brother Eric had died suddenly at age 57. We were stunned and grieved. Death is so final and so overwhelming. Paul's words remind us that God too is grieved by the power of death—that's why He took its sting at the cross and killed death at the empty tomb. That's why Jesus wept at the tomb of His friend Lazarus— He could feel the pain that death was causing His friends. The resurrection tells us that God so loves us that He entered our pain to forever take away the agony of death.

For those who are in Christ, death brings us into the presence of God. Paul writes, "Absent from the body is present with the Lord" (2 Corinthians 5:8, KJV). Earthly death in Christ brings us again into perfect relationship with God. Death that would have been the door to eternal separation from God is now, through Christ, the restoration of life in relationship with God.

In chapter three we discussed death as the major consequence of the fall, and we spoke of cell rejuvenation. Such a concept sounds like science fiction, but scientists are telling us that they believe they may be able to at least extend our lives with what they are learning. I believe this evidence points toward the biblical revelation that we were intended to live forever and one day will, in the resurrected, uncorruptible body that God gives us for eternity.

Jesus said, "For God so loved the world that He gave His only begotten Son, that whoever believes in Him should not perish but have *everlasting life*" (John 3:16, NKJV).[44]

Speaking again of death, Paul writes that our "body is sown in corruption, it is raised in incorruption" (1 Corinthians 15:42). That is, we die in a corrupting body, but we are raised in a body that will never decay. John makes it clear in Revelation 21:4 that death will no longer be a part of our existence. We will live forever.

> [God] will wipe away every tear from their eyes. Death will be no more; grief, crying, and pain

---

[44] New King James Version of the Bible, Thomas Nelson, 1982.

will be no more, because the previous things
have passed away
Revelation 21:4

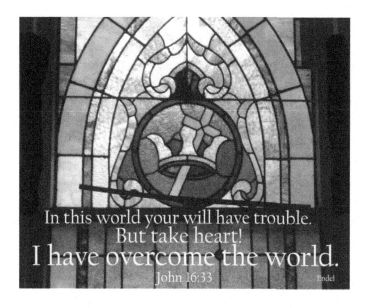

In this world your will have trouble.
But take heart!
I have overcome the world.
John 16:33   Endel

JESUS IS ABOUT HEALING RELATIONSHIPS

What do you know about Jesus? An increasing percentage
of our culture knows little to nothing about Jesus. They
hear His name as a curse word; they may even see His
form on a necklace, but they have never read His
biography from Matthew, Mark, Luke, or John.

Jesus is the most important man who has ever lived. He
sparked a spiritual fire two thousand years ago that
continues to blaze across the globe. History has been
separated by the years before Christ and the years after
Christ (BC—Before Christ; AD—Year of our Lord). His

execution was so public that hundreds of people witnessed of it. His resurrection was so convincing that those who proclaimed it died because they believed it was true, and within three hundred years there were believers all over the known world.

Many people do not believe in a God who would leave us in this broken world of suffering. I'm one of them. The Person of Jesus tells us that God did not leave us here to suffer endlessly, He came to set us free. God has come to man to offer us salvation from our suffering.

John's gospel begins by making it clear that Jesus was and always has been God. He was the Agent of creation. He came and took on human flesh to be among us. He lived His life perfectly in the balance of grace and truth. He suffered in this world of pain and injustice. He offered Himself in our place at the court of justice—the cross. He offers us forgiveness and spiritual healing through His act on our behalf. Through Him we can have an eternal relationship with God. He offers us peace with God and with each other.

Many people think Jesus was a good man and a great teacher, but when you read of Jesus' life and teachings, he doesn't leave that option. He was either Lord, liar, or lunatic. C. S. Lewis puts it this way:

"I am trying here to prevent anyone from saying the really foolish thing that people often say about Him [Jesus Christ]: 'I'm ready to accept Jesus as a great moral teacher, but I don't accept his claim to be God.' That is the one thing we must not say. A man who was merely a man and said the sort of things Jesus said would not be a great moral teacher. He would either be a lunatic—on a level with a man who says he is a poached egg—or else he would be the Devil of hell. You must make your choice. Either this man was, and is, the Son of God, or else a madman or something worse. You can shut him up for fool, you can spit at him and kill him as a demon; or you can fall at his feet and call him Lord and God. But let us not come up with any patronizing nonsense about his being a great human teacher. He has not left that option open to us. He did not intend to."

C. S. Lewis in Mere Christianity

Millions of people believe Christianity is about teachings, rules, and being good enough to get into heaven, but it's not. Biblical Christianity is about a relationship with Jesus Christ.

"Jesus saves" used to be a common expression in our culture, but I'm convinced most people have a superficial understanding of what it means. "Saves" is a common biblical term that can mean to be delivered or to be healed. One's soul can be saved or healed; one's body can be saved or healed. When we read of Jesus healing people, the word is much richer than just healing their physical disease, he heals their souls. This is consistent with the Hebrew concept of the person. The Greeks largely spoke of mankind as body, soul, and spirit. The Hebrew Bible acknowledges some division of human nature but primarily sees us as indivisible.

Christ offers to us the opportunity to be saved and healed from our sin and brokenness. Our bodies need to be fixed so we can live forever. Our minds need to be transformed so our broken thinking can be healed. Jesus wants us to live forever in perfect relationship with God and each other.

Jesus said, "I have come so that they may have life and have it in abundance" (John 10:10). He wants us to experience abundant life—full and rich in this world, but perfect and eternal in the next.

Giving your life to Jesus makes life in this world meaningful and the best it can be in this fallen and broken world. Further, it guarantees a perfect eternity in intimate fellowship with God. Life is all about relationships.

THE HOLY SPIRIT IS ABOUT RESTORING RELATIONSHIPS

The story is told about a little boy who was flying a kite. It was a windy day, and the kite kept going higher and higher. Finally, it got so high that it was out of sight. A man passed by and saw the little boy holding onto the string. The man could not see the kite, and he asked the boy, "How do you even know you have a kite up there?" The boy replied, "Because I can feel it."

Although we cannot see the Holy Spirit, we should be able to sense His work in our lives changing us into the image of Christ and drawing us together with other believers. We should sense Him protecting us from temptation. We should sense Him guiding us. We should sense Him revealing God and truth to us. We should sense Him filling us with joy even when times are tough. We should sense His voice when we read Scripture and pray.

The Holy Spirit is the third person of the Trinity. He lives within every believer (Romans 8:9). In many ways, our relationship with the Holy Spirit is the most intimate and mysterious of all relationships because the Holy Spirit lives in us. As Jesus prepared His disciples for his death and ultimate return to the Father in heaven, he spoke of the coming of the Holy Spirit who would be His presence in their lives. At its simplest, the Holy Spirit is the presence and power of God at work in the lives of every follower of Jesus.

Let me highlight just a few of the things that the Holy Spirit does in our lives:

1. He is the means of our conversion.
    Ephesians 1:13 says,

    > "you were also sealed with the promised Holy Spirit when you heard the world of truth, the gospel of your salvation, and when you believed."

2. He convicts us of sin and points us to Jesus (John 16:8-11).

3. He is a foretaste of what it will ultimately mean for us to fully realize our salvation in the new heaven and new earth (Revelation 21, 22) and He gives us evidence that we belong to God (Romans 8:16).

4. He fills us with joyful evidence of His presence. Is there a song in your heart? Are you grateful to the Lord? Do you follow God's will in all of your relationships?

    > "...be filled by the Spirit: speaking to one another in psalms, hymns, and spiritual songs, singing and making music with your heart in the Lord, giving thanks... submitting to one another in the fear of Christ" (Ephesians 5:18-21).

5. He gives us spiritual gifts with which to serve fellow believers in the church (1 Corinthians 12 and Romans 12).

6. He empowers us for godly living and mission (Acts 1:8) and convicts us of sin (Acts 2).

7. He teaches us the things of God (John 14:26, 16:13).

8. He helps us pray (Romans 8:26 and Ephesians 6:18).

9. He guides us through life (Acts 13:2).

10. He is the life-changing presence of God who makes us sensitive to sin and purifies our lives. He produces in us the "fruit of the Spirit": love, joy, peace, patience, kindness, goodness, faithfulness, gentleness, and self-control (Galatians 5:22-23). He makes us more like Jesus (see Chapter 14).

11. He makes us one with other followers of Jesus (John 17, 1 Corinthians 12:13, Ephesians 4:3). The Holy Spirit unites the people of God and makes us one, just as Jesus had asked of the Father.

Questions for Discussion

1. Was anything in this chapter new or helpful to you?
2. In what ways is the Bible all about relationships?
3. What are the five major steps necessary to see and understand what God is doing in the narrative of the Bible?
4. How does the law help us relationally?
5. What did Jesus do to make it possible for us to be brought into relationship with God and with each other?
6. Do you know what it means to have a relationship with Jesus?
7. What does the Holy Spirit do?
8. Where do you sense the Holy Spirit at work in your life?

Joyful, Joyful, We Adore Thee

Joyful, joyful, we adore You,
God of glory, **Lord of love;**
Hearts unfold like flow'rs before You,
Op'ning to the sun above.
Melt the clouds of sin and sadness;
Drive the dark of doubt away;
Giver of immortal gladness,
Fill us with the light of day!

Always giving and forgiving,
Ever blessing, ever blest,
Well-spring of the joy of living,
Ocean-depth of happy rest!
Loving Father, Christ our Brother,
Let Your light upon us shine;
Teach us how to love each other,
Lift us to the joy divine.

Mortals, join the mighty chorus,
Which the morning stars began;
God's own love is reigning o'er us,
Joining people hand in hand.
Ever singing, march we onward,
Victors in the midst of strife;
Joyful music leads us sunward
In the triumph song of life.

Words by Henry Van Dyke, Tun by Ludwig van Beethoven

GOD'S LOVE IS ABOUT RELATIONSHIPS

Love, like friendship, is not easily defined. I love ice cream; I love my dog, Bailey; I love my wife; I love God. A word broad enough to describe the diversity of these relationships needs explanation to bring precision. It is even harder for us to think about how God loves us, yet the Bible tells us that "God is love" (1John 4:8).

Two biblical words help us understand what God's love is. *Hesed* and *agape* dominate the teachings of the Bible. Both words, though from differing languages, have a richness that helps us understand the unfathomable depth of God's love.

First, the Hebrew word, *hesed,* richly incorporates many concepts into one word. It is used around 250 times in the Old Testament and is translated in various ways: love, loving kindness, faithfulness, mercy, loyalty, or steadfast love. *Hesed* love is unconditional love. *Hesed* is extravagant love. God gives it to us even though we are never worthy. *Hesed* love is the basis for God's greatest act in human history—the cross. At the cross, God displays the indefinable depth and breadth of His boundless love.

The second word is the Greek word, *agape*. *Agape* love was an underutilized Greek word that some theologians believe the Apostle Paul latched onto because it came closest to describing the kind of love God displays in Jesus. *Agape* love is a giving of ourselves over to someone; it is a commitment of our will and our life to another human being; it is to find our fulfillment in someone else's well-being. *Agape* love values someone else over our own self-interest. *Agape* love gives!

At the cross, God displayed His *hesed* and *agape* love, as Jesus was nailed to a cross to redeem us from our sin and brokenness. The Creator, Eternal King of the Universe suffered for us! He did it to solve our greatest problem, our guilt from sin, our sentence of death. He did it so we might have forgiveness and eternal life. He did it because He loves us.

Jesus died because of God's love for everyone—God's love for you. What more could God do to show His love for you. Jesus, Himself said it this way, "No one has greater love than this: to lay down his life for his friends" (John 15:13). Are you waiting for an engraved love letter from God to prove His love for you? At the cross, you have it. Engraved with nails and written in blood, God shouts from the cross, "I love you."

The Apostle John explains it this way:

God's love was revealed among us in this way: God sent his one and only Son into the world so that we might live through him. Love consists in this: not that

161

we loved God, but that he loved us and sent his Son
to be the atoning sacrifice for our sins. 1 John 4:9-10

Jesus died for you!
What more could God do
to show His love for you?

Paul shows us that God loves us despite our sin, "But God
proves his own love for us in that while we were still
sinners, Christ died for us" (Romans 5:8).

But God loves us too much to leave us in our sin. God
knows sin has broken us and thwarts us from peace,
fulfillment, and joy. His forgiveness is the beginning of
His process to set you free from sin. He doesn't just love
us once and leave us in our cesspool; He loves us enough
to help us get out of the sewage, get cleaned up, and
never go back.

Are you waiting for an engraved love letter
from God to prove His love for you?
At the cross, you have it.
Engraved with nails and written in blood,
God shouts from the cross, "I love you!"

Paul ends his first letter to the Thessalonians:

Now may the God of peace himself sanctify you [make you holy] completely. And may your whole spirit, soul, and body be kept sound and blameless at the coming of our Lord Jesus Christ. He who calls you is faithful; he will do it.
1 Thessalonians 5:23-24

The entire Bible is about God lovingly bringing us back to Himself. Through every step of mankind's story, God is loving us through creation, through the fall, through the law, through Christ, and into heaven!

- God loved us when He created us to be in perfect relationship with Himself and each other.
- God loved us when we sinned against Him by protecting us from eternal separation.
- God loved us by giving us the law which would guide us and protect us from each other.
- God loved us when he came to this earth, took on our pain, taught us, and died for us at the cross.

163

- God will love us for eternity in the restored perfection of Eden—the new heaven and the new earth. He loves us!

Remember John 3:16, "For God **so loved** the world that **he gave...**" God loved us by giving Himself through His Son, Jesus. Everything you need to know about God's love you can learn from Jesus. "My command is this: Love each other as I have loved you" (John 15:12).

Questions for Discussion

1. Define biblical love.
2. Scripture tells us that God is love (1 John 4:17). What does that mean?
3. What does the cross tell us about the love of God?
4. How has God loved us as revealed by the Bible?
5. Have you experienced the love of God?
6. Where can you see the love of God?

OUR LOVE FOR GOD
IS ABOUT RELATIONSHIPS

What does it mean for us to love God? How can we love God? To love God is to totally surrender ourselves to Him. Again, God loved us by giving Himself to us. We too, love God by giving ourselves to Him. "We love because he first loved us" (1 John 4:19).

The Bible tells us numerous times to "love God with all our hearts..." (Deuteronomy 6:5, Mark 12:28-31, Matthew 22:37-38, Luke 10:27). What does this mean?

Jesus lays the theological groundwork in Mark 12:28-31:

> One of the scribes approached. When he heard them debating and saw that Jesus answered them well, he asked him, "Which command is the most important of all?" Jesus answered, "The most important is Listen, O Israel! The Lord our God, the Lord is one. Love the Lord your God with all your heart, with all your soul, with all your mind, and with all your strength. The second is, Love your neighbor as yourself. There is no other command greater than these."

Jesus shares with us the perimeters of love—the more practical side of what it looks like to love God and to love others. Each phrase reveals the impact of love. To love God means to be fully devoted to Him with all our passion, with all our being, with all our thinking, with all our effort.

With all your heart—all your desire/passion
With all your soul—with all your being
With all your mind---with all your thinking
With all your strength—with all your effort

What can we do to express our love for God? Suppose you are a young man in love with a young woman. How would you show your love for her? Likely, you would seek out opportunities to be with her, you would tell her that you love her and receive her love. You'd want to know everything about her, so you'd study her, listen to her, and talk with her. You'd do the things you know she likes to do, and you'd try not to offend her by doing things she wouldn't like. You'd tell her all the things you love about her, and you'd tell your friends how wonderful she is!

You can do the same things in expression of your love for God.

- Seek Him. (Jeremiah 29:113). "Draw near to God, and he will draw near to you" (James 1:47).
- Acknowledge His Love (1 John 4:7).
- Know Him by Reading His Word (Psalm 119).
- Obey His Word "If you love me you will keep my commandments" (John 14:15).
- Worship Him (Psalm 95:6).
- Praise Him publicly (Psalm 150).

Let's now examine some of the practical ways we can love God.

HOW DO WE LOVE GOD? WE WORSHIP HIM!

Perhaps no greater area of confusion faces the modern church than worship. Many people think that worship is what we do when we sing; certainly, that is one aspect of worship, but worship is so much more than singing. Worship is adoring the greatness of God.

Worship is about our relationship with God and about our relationship with our fellow worshipers. When we worship with other believers, we seek relationship with God and with His people.

If we go to a baseball game and our team is batting in the bottom of the ninth inning, down by one with a man on first and two outs, and then the designated hitter steps up to the plate, as cool as a cucumber, and drives the ball completely out of the park to win the game, we are out of our minds with excitement! The sportscasters grab an interview with the hero as the crowd stands in awe; they praise him for coming through with the clutch homerun.

How much more ought our worship services draw us into amazement with God as he teaches us about Himself and receives our praise? How can we ignore the Hero of our faith? How can we not praise the One who has forgiven our sins and provided for our needs? How can we not praise Him for how He has spoken to us over this past week? He deserves our praise and worship. We were created for Him! We need to give Him glory!

How can we sleep through the sermon and mutter unemotional words of praise? We are together in the presence of God! How can we not be excited?
Worship is not about what we like, but about God and our relationship with Him. Emotionally charged services can become the object of our praise. Heady theological discussions can leave us wondering if we have talked about God but have not been with God.

Certainly not every worship service is exuberant, but Psalm 100 helps us to understand that worship is primarily about being with God. Notice the focus upon God in Psalm 100. I have bolded references to Him.

Let the whole earth shout
triumphantly to the Lord!
Serve the Lord *with gladness*;
come before **him** with *joyful songs*.
Acknowledge that **the** Lord **is God**.
He made us, and *we are* **his**
his people, the sheep of **his** pasture.
Enter **his** gates with *thanksgiving*
and **his** courts with *praise*.
Give thanks to **him** and bless **his name**.
For the Lord is good,
and **his** faithful love endures forever;
his faithfulness, through all generations.
Psalm 100

Worship is also about us relating to Him. Now go back and notice the italicized words that describe our part in worship. We are active in worship responding to the greatness of our God. We are in relationship with Him, speaking to Him and hearing from Him.

Shouting triumphantly to the LORD (v1)
Serving the LORD with gladness (v2)
Coming before Him with joyful songs (v2)
Acknowledging that the LORD is God (v3)
Entering His gates with thanksgiving (v4)
Entering His courts with praise (v4)
Giving thanks to Him (v4)
Blessing His name! (v5)

I am struck by how the Psalm weaves us into a relationship of celebration, joy, and love with God. When we worship together, we are loving God.

Worship is primarily about being with God!

HOW DO WE LOVE GOD?
WE LEARN TO TALK WITH GOD

Prayer and Bible reading go hand in hand. When we read and pray, we communicate with God. God primarily speaks through His Word. On the one hand, as you read the Bible, God is speaking to you; on the other hand, as you pray, you are speaking and then listening to God. This ongoing conversation is overseen by the Spirit of God who draws us together in intimate relationship.

The Holy Spirit, who is Himself God, and inspired men to write down God's Word, is our relational escort with God. He takes the Word and makes it alive to us. He applies it to our lives personally and helps us see and understand life from God's perspective. He speaks into the details of our lives.

Years ago, I was struggling to imagine how our little church could financially build the two buildings we believed God had placed on our hearts to build. We were growing, and God had dramatically worked to show us that we needed two buildings, not just one. Suddenly, the financial hurdle was much bigger, and I was struggling with standing before our congregation and saying, "I believe God wants us to step forward in faith and build these two buildings." Our congregation was to meet on Wednesday night to make the decision. I knew in my heart that if I led the church to do this that they would, but I was struggling. I couldn't lead God's people to do what I was not yet convinced was God's plan.

I often studied and prayed in the café court of the local mall because all the noises quietly focused me and helped me concentrate. I was working through Henry Blackaby's work entitled, *Experiencing God* and found God's timing to be amazing. He was discussing the crisis of faith that comes when we have heard from God but now must act in faith. As Blackaby led me through Scripture I could sense my confidence building. God would provide for what he called us to build. I paused and began to pray a prayer of thanksgiving for God's guidance and His patience with me. I was convinced. As I said, "Amen" I suddenly became aware of the mall music. It was the ending of the old Ray Orbison song, *You Got It*.

Anything you want, you got it
Anything you need, you got it
Anything at all, you got it.

The hair stood up on the back of my neck. God had spoken to me in His Word; He had confirmed it in prayer and then He put icing on the cake in the circumstances of the moment. I knew this was no game within my mind; I had been with God.

Photo by Eddy-Morton, Purchased on Lightstock.com

If you want to have a vibrant love relationship with God start first by reading His Word! I recommend that you begin reading in the gospel of John. There you will meet

Jesus, and later in the book, be introduced to the work of the Holy Spirit in the life of a believer.

Years ago, a friend of mine had grown up in a church that talked a little about Jesus but was not firmly committed to living out biblical teachings. A woman gave him a copy of the gospel of John and challenged him to read it. At the time, he was an angry rebellious young man who had rejected the Bible. For some reason he decided to do as she had asked, disprove the myths about Jesus, and then have nothing else to do with God or the church. By the time he had finished reading through John 3 he had become a believer!

Most people who have rejected Christianity have never read the Bible. To make matters worse, many Christians have not seriously engaged in personally reading the Bible. The Bible is not easy to read without some guidance. This is the reason that so many study Bibles and devotional Bibles have been introduced in the last five decades. Even for the experienced reader, these are extremely helpful.[45]

When you first start reading the Bible, you don't have the context of its flow from creation to heaven. Usually you are better able to understand the New Testament then go back and read the Old Testament.

---

[45] There are many excellent study Bibles available today. I continue to use the NIV Study Bible, the CSB Study Bible, and the ESV Study Bible. Additionally, I have recommended the Life Application Bible to people new to Bible study. I also recommend Our Daily Bread devotionals available through an app on your phone or on the internet at odb.org.

I have found it helpful to understand the Bible by tracing these five major events through Scripture:

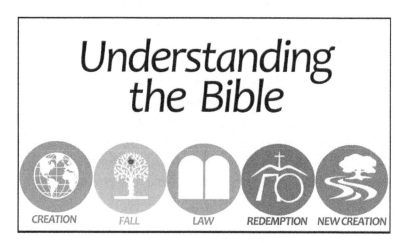

Creation: God is the eternal Creator who created the heavens and the earth based upon His perfect attributes. Mankind was created in His image and given the opportunity to rebel against God which allowed mankind the real option of loving God.

Fall: Adam and Even unleashed sin upon mankind and the creation when they rebelled against God's expressed will. The devasted and broken world that we live in today was the result.

Law: God provided mankind the law to point us to the best way to live as broken people in a broken world. His rules are designed to protect us from ourselves and each other. They become helpful to our survival, but broken as we are, we could never live them perfectly. God knew this. God primarily introduced the law in the Torah or the first five books of the Old Testament. Much of the remaining Old Testament describes God's people attempting to live under the teachings of the law or the Torah. They were unable to fulfill the law, but God had a plan for changing their broken hearts. The law showed us how desperately we need Jesus. The New Testament shows us God's plan.

Redemption: In the New Testament, God entered humanity in the person of Jesus, lived among us perfectly, and then died on a cross satisfying the justice of a holy God with His own love for us. God paid the just price for our sin and offers forgiveness to those who believe in what Jesus did at the cross. Today we enjoy the beginning of redemption, while in the process of being healed but still living in a fully broken world, we long for our ultimate healing in the new heaven and the new earth.

New Creation: Through the resurrection, death is conquered and is transformed into the doorway into eternity where God's new heaven and new earth await us as new creatures in Christ. No longer broken people living in a broken world, we become perfect people living in a perfect world for eternity.

When you begin to understand the big picture of the Bible, you can read and hear from God. Understanding these major events help you to process the details of this cohesive and amazing Book. His Spirit will help you and draw you as you seek a vibrant relationship with God. When you read the Bible, you are loving God.

HOW DO WE LOVE GOD?
WE LIVE HIS WAY

Jesus said in John 14:21, "If you love me, you will keep my commandments." One way that we love God is by doing what He tells us to do—living life His way.

God's Word is more than an owner's manual. When I bought my car, inside the glove compartment was a little book that told me all the things I needed to do to extend the life of my vehicle. If I wanted the best out of my car, I needed to change the oil every 7,000 miles, I needed the belts inspected and adjusted a couple months after I began driving the car. I needed to rotate the tires every 10,000 miles. You know the routine. God's Word is like an owner's manual, it describes the best way to live life in this fallen world.

But our relationship with God cannot be fully understood as an owner's manual, more importantly, it is a covenant of relationship. When we get married, we promise to each other certain behavior as an expression of our love. We promise to take care of each other, we promise to be faithful to each other, we promise to give priority to each other. We love each other by living up to our promises and serving each other to the best of our abilities.

Likewise, we love God by serving Him and each other according to His good desires for us. We do what is right out of our love for God. We don't want to offend a holy God by rebelliously demanding our own way. That would be like telling your wife you love her and then having an affair with another woman! We know and understand that

God has our best interests at heart. He tells us how to live because He knows what's best for us. We love Him by trusting Him and believing that His way is the best for us. As Jesus said, "if you love me you will do what I command" (John 14:15).

When you do what God's Word tells you to do, you are loving God.

HOW DO WE LOVE GOD? WE LIVE FOR HIS GLORY!

What is this life about? I have come to accept the wisdom of the Westminster Catechism: "Man's chief end is to glorify God, and to enjoy Him forever." John Piper adds this perspective, "God is most glorified in us when we are most satisfied in Him."[46] What does it mean to glorify God and enjoy Him? It means that life's ultimate purpose is about rightly relating to God and bringing glory to Him through how we live.

When Sarah and I got engaged we went to a photographer for an engagement picture. I carried that picture with me for years; the picture was published in the newspaper announcing our engagement. I wanted everyone to know how wonderful my fiancé was. Today, couples do elaborate picture collages on Facebook with a beautiful diamond ring. The point is the same, "Look at my wonderful fiancé!"

---

[46] John Piper, *Desiring God—Meditations of a Christian Hedonist,* (Colorado Springs: Multinomah Books, 2011), Kindle Edition.

In a similar way, when you get to know God you want others to know how wonderful He is. In Bible language, you are declaring His glory!

Giving glory to God sounds a bit strange to most of us. There are only about ten superlative words that we can use to describe Him and soon these words lose their power. The wonder rubs off of them and we become unable to express His glory. Words simply fall short.

I remember pondering this God who was so concerned about His glory that He commanded us to praise Him. If a boy down the street demanded praise, I would think him vain and egotistical. Why is God any different?

Well, for one thing, God is the only being worthy of superlative praise. He is the center of all things. All that we see and know is an extension of His creative power and wisdom. "There is no one like Him" to use the wording of a current praise song. He is so much more than we can see or imagine that there is nothing to compare Him to.

Most of you have attended plenty of firework shows. Nothing really changes from year to year. They are mostly the same colors, the same noises, and similar combinations, but we still get excited. I have stood and watched people as they watched the fireworks. Their eyes light up and the corners of their lips raise up in a smile. I have watched the most stoic of people lightly gasp with amazement. I find watching people's reactions to the fireworks more fun than the actual show!

Here's the thing. When we catch a glimpse of Almighty God, we can't help but praise Him. Further, God comes near to us when we praise Him, "God inhabits the praises of His People" (Psalm 22:3)! He shows His glory so that we might experience His glory and reflect His glory to others! As we experience His glory we are blessed and awed by His presence. We encounter God.

What appears to be a command by a vain God who insatiably needs our praise is really a command designed to bring us into His presence, experience His glory, and be transformed into His likeness. In Him we will experience His peace and unspeakable joy! God's command for us to praise Him is really a call for us to enter His joy! We are the ones who are blessed when we enter His courts with praise (Psalm 100:4).

The more we are tuned into the glory of God the more we want to live consistently out of who He is and how He has revealed Himself to us. We want our lives to declare His glory. When we declare His glory, we are loving God.

Questions for Discussion

1. In what ways do you love God?
2. Do you focus on God in worship or do you primarily focus on you and your needs?
3. How might you include Bible study and prayer in your life?
4. Share a time or a memory in which you believe that God clearly spoke to a need in your life.
5. What does it mean to give God glory? How can you give glory to God?

LOVING PEOPLE IS ABOUT RELATIONSHIPS

Once you've experienced the love of God then you will have the capacity to begin to love people. If you love God, you will begin to love people. This is proof of our growing love for God.

> If anyone says, "I love God," and yet hates his brother or sister, he is a liar. For the person who does not love his brother or sister whom he has seen cannot love God whom he has not seen. And we have this command from him: The one who loves God must also love his brother and sister.
> 1 John 4:20-21

VARIOUS TYPES OF LOVE

In a tender embrace the young man proclaims his love for her, but does he really love her? What does that mean anyway? What passes for love in our culture is generally conditional love. If you live up to my expectations, I'll "love" you. If you give me what I want, then I will love you. "I love you" can be so twisted that it often means, "I love myself and you give me what I want to make me happy." That's not biblical love. That's self-centeredness. Such transactional love really is not love at all—it's really just love of self. We "love" someone for what they do for us. If they quit performing to our expectations, we don't "love" them anymore. Such is the failure of many marriages.

As we have seen, the Bible defines love differently than our culture does. Agape love is about giving ourselves over to someone. It is a commitment of our will and our life to someone. It is a willingness to give up ourselves for the good of another. Love gives itself, its time, its devotion, its attention, its everything to the beloved. Love values the beloved; love strives to please the beloved; love serves the beloved. Love values someone else over our own self-interest. Such love is difficult and rare.

People are messed up and hard to love. We're like porcupines trying to connect, but we keep poking each other and repulsing each other.

Jesus teaches us how to love others by building on a rich tradition of biblical and Jewish thought regarding human relationships. I have found it helpful to understand His extraordinary teaching on love by following several steps of thinking: the Silver Rule, the Golden Rule, and finally, Jesus's ultimate statement of love, what I call the Platinum Rule.

The Silver Rule is a negative statement of the Golden Rule, "Do not do unto others as you would have them do unto you." According to tradition, the Silver Rule was articulated in the first century BC and associated with the development of the Jewish Mishnah and the Talmud, a sort of commentary on the Torah and its law.

Jesus stated the Golden Rule in Matthew 7:12, "Therefore, whatever you want others to do for you, do also the same for them, for this is the Law and the Prophets." It has popularly been rendered, "Do unto others as you would have them do unto you." As profound as this teaching is, it is not the pinnacle of Jesus' teaching on love.

When Sarah and I bought our first house we were reminded of another condescending Golden Rule. Our realtor was struggling to show us houses we could afford, so she reminded us of the Golden Rule. I was puzzled, but it hit me a few minutes later. Her Golden Rule was "He who has the gold rules." We didn't have the gold! This rule is certainly not about love.

Jesus further expanded our understanding of love when he said, "Love you neighbor as yourself." I've heard people say this means we are to love ourselves. That was not Jesus' point. We naturally look out for ourselves; Jesus wanted us to understand our obligation to look out for our neighbors—to be our brother's keeper. Too many of us are physically mature but emotionally three-year-olds who believe the world revolves around us. Jesus reminds us that we are to care as much about our neighbors as we do about ourselves.

In Matthew 5:43-44 Jesus expands this call to love in an extraordinary way:

"You have heard that it was said, Love your neighbor and hate your enemy. But I tell you, love your enemies and pray for those who persecute you, so that you may be children of your Father in heaven. For he causes his sun to rise on the evil and the good, and sends rain on the righteous and the unrighteous. For if you love those who love you, what reward will you have? Don't even the tax collectors do the same? And if you greet only your brothers and sisters, what are you doing out of the ordinary? Don't even the Gentiles do the same? Be perfect, therefore, as your heavenly Father is perfect.

Love your enemy! Are you kidding? I call this the Platinum Rule because it is the ultimate measure of love. Doing unto others as they do for you is just good business. It's a good transaction but that's all. If you don't love me in return, then I won't love you.

Jesus spoke about and illustrated real love in Romans 5:8, "But God proves his own love for us in that while we were still sinners, Christ died for us." That's the Platinum Rule in action. The Platinum Rule is not for sissies! It takes character of steel to live like this. That's exactly what Jesus showed us at the cross, "Father, forgive them for they know not what they do" (Luke 23:34).

Peter reminds us of the power of love, "Above all, maintain constant love for one another, since love covers a multitude of sins (1 Peter 4:8).

Paul's ultimate definition of love is found in 1 Corinthians 13:

Love is patient, love is kind. Love does not envy, is not boastful, is not arrogant, is not rude, is not self-seeking, is not irritable, and does not keep a record of wrongs. Love finds no joy in unrighteousness but rejoices in the truth. It bears all things, believes all things, hopes all things, endures all things. Love never ends.

WHO ARE WE TO LOVE?

We are expected to even love our enemies! Let's make it even harder, we're supposed to love everyone! Most Americans know the term, "good Samaritan," but fewer know the story and its concluding application. The Samaritans were looked down upon as inferior people. Jesus masterfully made them the unlikely heroes to strengthen His point:

[A man asked Jesus] "And who is my neighbor?" Jesus took up the question and said, "A man was going down from Jerusalem to Jericho and fell into the hands of robbers. They stripped him, beat him up, and fled, leaving him half dead. A priest happened to be going down that road. When he saw him, he passed by on the other side. In the same way, a Levite, when he arrived at the place and saw him, passed by on the other side. But a Samaritan on his journey came up to him, and when he saw the man, he had compassion. He went over to him and bandaged his wounds, pouring on olive oil and wine. Then he put him on his own animal, brought him to an inn, and took care of him. The next day he took out two denarii, gave them to the innkeeper, and said, 'Take care of him. When I come back, I'll reimburse you for whatever extra you spend.' "Which of these three do you think proved to be a neighbor to the man who fell into the hands of the robbers?" "The one who showed mercy to him," he said. Then Jesus told him, "Go and do the same." Luke 10:29-37

Jesus' point is that everyone is my neighbor! Every opportunity God presents us is an opportunity to love someone. You might not know the starving child in South America, but God brings a missionary to your church and gives you an opportunity. You might not know the family with the picture on the medical gift jar at your grocery store, but God has invited you to love? Who are you to love? Everyone you meet on life's journey.

HOW ARE WE TO LOVE?

Jesus must have had the teaching of Micah 6:8 in His mind as He answered the man's question.

He has shown you, O man, what is good;
And what does the LORD require of you
but to do justly, to love mercy,
and to walk humbly with your God?

The Samaritan was moved by his compassion. He did what was right (do justly) and showed mercy to the wounded man. He then set aside his plans (walk humbly with your God) to minister as God gave him opportunity.

From time to time God puts us all in situations and presents us with the opportunity to care for someone, to show them mercy, to give generously. These opportunities are invitations from God to love someone in a tangible way. I am often so busy that I feel the temptation to let the moment pass. Someone once told me, "If you're too busy to help people, then you're too busy." I've discovered that even the busiest of us do what we really want to do.

How Are We to Love?
Love by Giving Yourself to Others
Love by Listening to Others
Love by Being Kind & Compassionate
Love by Sharing Other's Burdens
Love by Encouraging Others
Love by Praying for Others
Love by Being Generous to Others
Love by Telling Others the Truth
Love by Working for Justice
Love by Forgiving Others
Love by Sharing Jesus

How Are We to Love?
Love by Giving Yourself to Others

We often relish the good times and emotions of love forgetting just how challenging love can be. Love is glorious, but love is also expensive. Back in Chapter Nine we defined love and noticed that "Love Gives."

Love gives!

As we begin thinking about how we can love others we must be honest that loving others will cost us. There are times when love is very expensive; love cost Jesus His life. Love will cost you time, money, worry, conflict, etc. Love is often challenging. Few parents ever imagine how much their love will cost them when they hold their sweet newborn child, but talk to the parent of a teenager, and most can tell you how much it costs to love.

Love is often terribly inconvenient. People don't schedule their struggles to match your schedule. When they need you, dishes will go unwashed, laundry undone, the grass will be three days overdue, you'll get less sleep, and deadlines will be missed. Love will often take time that you don't have and steal your peace of mind. Love gives.

Often, the greatest gift we give others is our time. My wife got a copied text message this morning about a little girl's upcoming birthday. She said, "All I want for my birthday is to be with Abbie." Wow! Love others by giving yourself, and your time, to them.

Love by Listening to Others

One of the best ways to love people is to listen to them. For most of us, this is more challenging than it might first appear. Some of us are talkers and lousy listeners. Some of us have short attention spans and are easily distracted. Some of us are so caught up in ourselves that we simply don't care that much about other people. Most of us underestimate the value of deeply listening to others.

Bill Tinsley taught me the importance of listening when we began pastor/peer learning groups in 2011. Each pastor was given more than an hour to tell their story without any interruption; one pastor spoke for almost three hours! What happened was astounding. In less than twenty-four hours these men grew to love each other, encourage each other, and support each other. A group of eight men we thought would meet for a year, have voluntarily set aside busy schedules for over six years.

Most of us enjoy telling our story; we feel cared for when someone cares enough to listen. It is satisfying and draws us to other people, we are affirmed and loved. We're delighted and connected when we hear things that resonate with us, experiences that sound like our own. We feel their pain when they share the painful moments of their lives.

If you want to love someone well, learn to listen to them. It takes practice and discipline, but it is a powerful way to love.

> *If you judge people,*
> *you have no time to love them.*
> *Mother Teresa*

Love by Being Kind
and Compassionate to Others

Bad manners, impatience, vulgarity, and rudeness are all around us. How refreshing to be agents of kindness, patience, and compassion. Our interactions with people can be cold, impersonal, and curt. How refreshing is a word of kindness.

The Bible is full of verses that tell us to "be kind and compassionate to each other" (Ephesians 4:32). "But the fruit of the Spirit is... kindness" (Galatians 5:22). "Therefore, God's chosen ones, holy and loved, put on heartfelt compassion, kindness..." (Colossians 3:12). "Love is kind" (1 Corinthians 13:4).

Being kind to others carries a double blessing. Generally speaking, people respond back in gentleness and you are blessed. The kind person finds himself/herself living in a kind world, "A kind man benefits himself..." (Proverbs

11:17). "A generous person will prosper; whoever refreshes others will be refreshed" (Proverbs 11:25, NIV).

Kind words are free.

Love by Sharing Other's Burdens

When Sarah and I lost our first child, life was a painful blur. Friends and family gathered around us and helped us put together a graveside service and prayed for us. People helped us by carrying us through this difficult time. Friends organized a gospel music night and took up an offering that helped us tremendously with all the expenses. I have often times looked back on that experience as a time when others helped carry our burden.

All of us go through times of struggle and pain; we all fall down occasionally. It's so encouraging to know that we have friends and family who are there to help us when we are barely making it. The writer of Ecclesiastes noted this:

"Two are better than one... For if either falls, his companion can lift him up; but pity the one who falls without another to lift him up" (Ecclesiastes 4:10).

The Apostle Paul wrote, "Carry one another's burdens; in this way you will fulfill the law of Christ" (Galatians 6:2).

189

Some people worry that they don't have the magic words to help someone in pain, and honestly, they don't. The ministry of presence is often the greatest thing you can give to someone who is hurting. A hot cup of coffee and an open, nonjudgmental ear which will listen to someone processing pain can be the greatest thing you can do for a friend. Don't think you can heal their pain with pious theological platitudes. Ask for God to comfort them in their pain. Listen and then pray for them.

So many times, when I was stressed and times were tough, I have been encouraged by the presence of a friend. In the words of the old Beatle's song, "We get by with a little help from our friends."

Love by Encouraging Others

The New Testament speaks frequently of God's command for us to encourage one another; in fact, the term appears 105 times in the New Testament. It means to "come alongside" someone and share with them what they need to meet the challenges of life.

> 1 Thessalonians 5:11, Therefore encourage one another and build each other up as you are already doing.

Encouragement is so powerful and so easy to do that one wonders, "Why don't we encourage others more?" Why don't we become "sons of encouragement" like Barnabas was called by the early church?

> And let us consider one another in order to provoke love and good works, not neglecting to gather together, as some are in the habit of doing, but encouraging each other, and all the more as you see the day approaching.
> Hebrews 10:24-25

Note that Paul expects us to gather regularly for worship where we will naturally encourage each other. Christians gathering together reminds us that we are not alone. When we need encouragement, someone there has been sent by God to provide it. When someone else needs encouragement, we might be God's encouraging word to them. When praising God together and striving to live for Jesus we find what we need from each other.

Modern technology has made it relatively easy for us to connect and encourage each other. I'm surprised that we don't send more encouraging text messages or leave more affirming comments on Facebook. Most of us live our lives with our eyes on ourselves and the world three feet in front of us. Being the answer to someone else's need can be one of the greatest blessings in life.

We all have tough days and difficult seasons of life. When we are discouraged, it is amazing how a kind word or a hug resets us at a lower level of anxiety. You have the power to encourage almost anyone with a kind word. Please, encourage someone today!

Love by Praying for Others

An email just popped up on my computer screen as I moved to this paragraph. Norman, an old friend who lives 700 miles away, just read our church email and typed me a note, "We pray for you and for Emmanuel and for the MWBC Executive Committee Meeting (taking place tonight) and for the State Missions Offering." Wow! How wonderful to know that others know your struggles are lifting you up in prayer.

The Bible makes it clear that we should pray for each other:

> James 5:16, Therefore, confess your sins to one another and pray for one another, so that you may be healed. The prayer of a righteous person is very powerful in its effect.

> 1 Timothy 2:1, First of all, then, I urge that petitions, prayers, intercessions, and thanksgivings be made for everyone,

Ephesians 6:18, Pray at all times in the Spirit with every prayer and request, and stay alert with all perseverance and intercession for all the saints.

> *A spontaneous, short, sincere prayer says, "I love you" louder than almost anything else!*

Colossians 1:9, For this reason also, since the day we heard this, we haven't stopped praying for you. We are asking that you may be filled with the knowledge of his will in all wisdom and spiritual understanding.

The power of God is released into the lives of His people when we pray. A quick prayer often settles down the most traumatized and upset. Don't just promise to pray, stop for fifteen seconds and pray the simplest prayer that God would meet their need and fill them with His peace. A spontaneous, short, sincere prayer says, "I love you" louder than almost anything else!

Love by Being Generous to Others

A rumpled man walks into a bank in New York City and asks for the loan officer. He says he is going to Europe on business for two weeks and needs to borrow $5,000. The bank officer says the bank will need some kind of security for such a loan. So, the man, clearly eccentric, hands over the keys to a new Rolls Royce parked on the street in front of the bank. Everything checks out, and the bank agrees to accept the car as collateral for the loan. An employee drives the Rolls into the bank's underground garage and parks it there. Two weeks later, the man returns, repays the $5,000 and the interest of $15.41. The loan officer says, "We are very happy to have had your business, and this transaction has worked out very nicely, but we are a little puzzled. While you were away, we checked you out and found that you are a multi-millionaire. What puzzles us is why would you bother to borrow $5,000?" The man replied, "Where else in New York could I park my car for two weeks for $15.41?

Disney's rendition of Ebenezer Scrooge as a miserable miser was perfect. He was so fixated on his money that he had no human compassion or connection at all. Most of us are not quite so tight or so miserable, but have we learned the ultimate lesson of Ebenezer Scrooge? There is life and joy in generosity.

There is so much joy in generosity that God's Word assures us that by blessing others we are blessed. Jesus even said, "It's more blessed to give than to receive" (Acts 20:35). Proverbs 11:25 gives insight here, "A generous person will prosper; whoever refreshes others will be refreshed." (NIV)

"Never resist a generous impulse."
O.S. Hawkins
President of GuideStone Financial Services

As I study the Bible and follow the example of God, I realize that loving is giving. "For God so loved the world that he gave..." (John 3:16). Love gives! Agape love, sacrificial love, challenges us to give ourselves away.

Here's an amazing secret I discovered years ago. I can give $100 to help someone and get $1000 worth of joy out of it! Weird, huh? Kind of, but I've found it to be true over and over again. God just does something special in your soul when He uses you to help meet someone's need.

Generosity isn't just about money. Share your life generously with others. Give them your time when they need someone to talk to. Give them your help when you can do something to meet their physical needs—cut their grass, shovel their snow, fix them a meal. Give whatever you have and whoever you are as broadly as God gives you the ability. Bake three of your favorite pies and give two away. Give your neighbors a craft if you're crafty. Pass out compliments and encouragement whenever you can. Offer hospitality as an act of compassion, encouragement, and ministry. Invite people into your home for a meal or dessert. Allow someone the use of your extra bedroom during a time of transition or need. Take someone out to coffee or lunch who is struggling personally or financially. Send a card and/or a gift card to encourage someone or help them. When people are hurting, most of us want to give!

Mother Teressa said, "This is the meaning of true love, to give until it hurts." Go ahead and love some people around you. Give until it hurts... beyond your ability. You can't out give God! Jesus said, "It is more blessed to give than receive" (Acts 20:35).

> *Giving is one way of saying,*
> *"I love you."*
>
> Endel

Love by Telling Others the Truth

Friends tell each other the truth. "Faithful are the wounds of a friend" (Proverbs 27:6). Jesus was "full of grace and truth" (John 1:15).

First, let me be clear that not everything needs to be said. You don't really like your friend's purple hair, but you don't need to say so. If he/she pushes you, you don't have to express your opinion. If they like it, be happy for them. I have a great cousin in her 80's with purple hair, and I've got to admit, I like it! But be careful, if your wife asks you if she looks fat in this dress, you'd better tell her the truth with grace. She can read your mind!

Paul helps us understand how to speak the truth with grace, humility, gentleness, and love in Ephesians 4:1, 15:

> Therefore I, the prisoner in the Lord, urge you to walk worthy of the calling you have received, with all humility and gentleness, with patience, bearing with

one another in love, making every effort to keep the unity of the Spirit through the bond of peace... But speaking the truth in love, let us grow in every way to him who is the head—Christ.

He adds in verse 25, "Therefore, putting away lying, speak the truth, each one to his neighbor, because we are members of one another."

When a painful truth must be shared, share it with love. Suppose your friend has a spat with one of your mutual acquaintances. Things were said and your friend mistreats the other person with an accusation or half-truth that you both know is not true. She's still in a flurry over what has happened, and she asks you, "Can you believe what she said to me?" Most of us will, out of loyalty, tend toward aligning ourselves with her position, but is that the right thing to do? Our friend was wrong on her facts, angry in her response, and dismissive, do we let that pass? Love her enough to gently show her the error of her ways. Do it with grace and truth.

Love by Working for Justice

So much pulls us apart in this world. We have been segmented and separated by sin and superficial differences such as skin color and economic status. The Bible speaks about justice. We must love by working for justice.

God is just. God is not a respecter of persons (Acts 10:34). He does not discriminate against people on the basis of anything other than our response to His Son. God loves us all and desires that we become one (John 17), but sin keeps us separated.

Here are few of the Scriptures that emphasize the importance of justice.

Do not act unjustly when deciding a case. Do not be partial to the poor or give preference to the rich; judge your neighbor fairly.
Leviticus 19:15

But you must return to your God; maintain love and justice...
Hosea 12:6

When justice is done, it brings joy to the righteous but terror to evildoers.
Proverbs 21:15

The righteous person knows the rights of the poor, but the wicked one does not understand these concerns.
Proverbs 29:7

He loves righteousness and justice; the earth is full of the LORD's unfailing love.
Psalm 33:5

Learn to do what is good. Pursue justice. Correct the oppressor. Defend the rights of the fatherless. Plead the widow's cause.
Isaiah 1:17

For I, the LORD, love justice;
I hate robbery and injustice;
I will faithfully reward my people
and make a permanent covenant with them.
Isaiah 61:8

The LORD of Armies says this:
"Make fair decisions. Show faithful love
and compassion to one another."
Zechariah 7:9

Our nation is today engaged in a civil war over justice. We have nuanced the battle lines to such a degree that we find it difficult to even talk to each other. Anger and violence are devastating our land.

Dr. Martin Luther King, Jr. was, and continues to be, one of the strongest voices for justice in history. He believed and articulated that justice would not come through violence, which would only continue to deeply divide us, but through love. As a pastor, he understood the power of the love that comes through the gospel of Jesus Christ. Many of Dr. King's best-known quotations emphasize this truth.

Love is the only force capable of
transforming an enemy into a friend.

Injustice anywhere
is a threat to justice everywhere.

Hatred paralyzes life; love releases it.
Hatred confuses life; love harmonizes it.
Hatred darkens life; love illuminates it.

Darkness cannot drive out darkness;
only light can do that.
Hate cannot drive out hate;
Only love can do that.

Love is the most durable power in the world.

We must learn to live together as brothers
or we will perish together as fools.

The great event on Calvary
signifies more than a meaningless drama
that took place on the stage of history.
It is a telescope through which
we look out into the long vista of eternity
and see the love of God breaking forth into time.

Was not Jesus an extremist in love?
'Love your enemies, bless them that curse you,
pray for them that despitefully use you.'

Love by Saying You're Sorry

The 70's stupid love sayings still pop up in my mind,
"Love means never having to say you're sorry."[47] That's
ridiculous! When you love someone, you want to quickly
say you're sorry. We are sinful human beings and we hurt
each other. Sometimes we don't even know when we
harm another; sometimes our sinfulness does it willfully.

---

[47] Erich Segal, Love Story, made popular in the 1970 film, Love Story.

200

When we wrong someone, we need to love them enough to fully say we're sorry.

Here are some steps to renew your love to someone you've wronged.

- First, quickly confess to them that what you said or did was wrong.

- If you need to explain what occurred, be careful not to excuse your action to shift away from yourself responsibility for what happened.

- Be specific about how you wronged them.

- Express what you understand about the pain this caused them.

- Don't make your apology conditional on their response.

- Be prepared to accept their anger without rebuttal. Remember that you have processed your apology; they have not, they're still one step behind you.

- Ask for forgiveness but give them time to process your apology. Sometimes people accept an apology too quickly; sometimes it takes hours or days for an apology to be fully accepted.

- Offer a way to make it right, if restitution is possible. "I did know there was a problem with the radiator on the car I sold you. I will pay to have it repaired."

Peter writes, "Above all, maintain constant love for one another, since love covers a multitude of sins" (1 Peter 4:8).

Love by Forgiving Others

Forgiveness is perhaps the most challenging concept in the universe! Even for God. The justice of God in tension with the love of God demanded a supernatural intervention by God Himself. It took God's personal immersion into our pain to solve the dilemma in Christ. We have all been wronged by someone—an unfaithful spouse or a parent? Abandoned or abused by a parent? Stabbed in the back? Betrayed, slandered, or betrayed by a friend? Cheated financially? Treated apathetically? Prejudiced, criticized, or judged? Manipulated? Sexually used? Ignored? Treated like trash? We have all been wronged!

> *"Forgiveness is man's deepest need and God's greatest accomplishment."*
>
> Horace Bushnell

Forgiveness means to "cancel a debt" or to pardon someone. It means to give up your right to get even with someone. To understand biblical forgiveness, we need to see it from two perspectives.

First, biblical forgiveness requires that we release the wrongdoer and trust God to handle justice and heal our suffering. God requires us to forgive one another. Even the guiltiest among us are only a little more guilty than we are.

The Bible speaks frequently and broadly to forgiveness:

- Romans 12:18, tells us to seek reconciliation.

- Romans 12:19, tells us to resist revenge.

- 1 Thessalonians 5:15, tell us to not return evil for evil.

- Matthew 5:44, tells us to pray for the welfare of the one who has wronged us.

- Exodus 23:4, tells us to aid those who have hurt us when they are in distress.

- Luke 17:3-4, tells us "If your brother sins, rebuke him, and if he repents, forgive him. And if he sins against you seven times in a day, and comes back to you seven times, saying, 'I repent,' you must forgive him."

- Jesus tells us, "love your enemies and pray for those who persecute you." Matthew 5:44

Forgiveness is complex and confusing:

- Forgiveness does not mean pretending that evil never took place.

- Forgiveness does not mean making excuses for someone's bad behavior.

- Forgiveness is allowing God to take care of justice.

- Forgiveness is not allowing the offense to recur again and again.

- Forgiveness is not the same as reconciliation.

- Forgiveness is usually a process not an event.

- Forgiveness does not mean forgetting.

- Forgiveness does not mean denying reality or ignoring repeated offenses.

- Forgiveness is not conditioned upon their repentance. We still need to forgive.

- Forgiveness is not based on other's action but on our attitude.

- Forgiveness does not necessarily have to be announced to the offender.

- Forgiveness begins with a decision to trust God.[48]

You might say that God doesn't forgive without confession and repentance and you would be correct. But we have not been wronged in the same way God has been wronged. God is holy and perfect. He is just; we are not. The core of His character is holy and cannot tolerate sin. His forgiveness brings eternal life. Our forgiveness is of limited scope and largely serves to set us free from our own bitterness. God's forgiveness is the offer to be absolved of sin. Our forgiveness simply overlooks the sin. God offers to remove the sin through paying the penalty Himself.

---

[48] Loosely based on a Focus on the Family article: https://www.focusonthefamily.com/marriage/forgiveness-and-restoration/

God is just and holy. We are not. He cannot simply overlook sin. His justice demands that our sin be judged. Either we receive the punishment we deserve, or God takes our punishment upon Himself, and we, by faith, claim the forgiveness that he has provided and offered.

Secondly, God's forgiveness is realized when we turn to Him in repentance and trust in the saving work of Jesus. His forgiveness is realized when we confess our sin and repent from our behavior. God's forgiveness requires confession and repentance.

Love by Sharing Jesus

The most loving thing that a follower of Jesus can do is to share the hope of forgiveness and healing that comes through Jesus Christ. In chapter three, we discussed the brokenness of this world and of humanity. Sin has left us wounded and hurting. Ultimately, we will all die and face the God of truth and grace. Even the American Dream is temporary and illusional. Under the surface we will all experience decline, disease, and death. All of us long for a greater purpose than just going through the motions of life... even if we are fortunate and they are mostly good.

Jesus told his disciples, "No one has greater love than this: to lay down his life for his friends" (John 15:13). Jesus' love for mankind took Him to the cross where the greatest injustice of human history became the greatest act of love in human history. He did not owe the penalty of death for His sins, but out of His love for each of us, He paid the penalty for our sin.

The Gospel is a love story. Out of love for us, God did the unthinkable, He took death, the penalty of sin, on Himself, suffered and died in our place. Then He conquered death when He stepped out of the tomb. He offers to us victory over sin through the cross and eternal life through the empty tomb. "Thanks be to God who gives us the victory through our Lord Jesus Christ" (1 Corinthians 15:57)! Share the love story of Jesus with the people you love.

> *The Gospel is a love story.*
> *Share the love story of Jesus*
> *with the people you love.*

Questions for Discussion

1. How do you most effectively love others?
2. Are there other ways you need to grow in your ability to love?
3. Who do you need to listen to?
4. Who do you need to encourage?
5. Are you generous in your love for others?
6. Who are you praying for?
7. How are love and justice connected?
8. Who do you need to forgive?
9. Is there someone in your life that you need to share the gospel with?

PERSONAL GROWTH
IS ABOUT RELATIONSHIPS

The Bible tells us that when we become believers in Jesus Christ, His Spirit comes to live within us. He begins to change us and make us more like Jesus. He begins to heal our brokenness.

Galatians 5 powerfully describes the natural state of fallen man and the person we can become through the power of the Holy Spirit. Paul marks out for us the works of the flesh. Among the sins listed is a group of sins that have been identified by commentators as relational sins: hatreds, strife, jealousy, outbursts of anger, selfish ambitions, dissensions, factions, and envy. As we grow in the Spirit, these sins, and the others listed, ought to be passing away in our lives. God wants to bring about in us growth in our ability to love others.

In contrast to the relational sins, Paul lists what has come to be called, The Fruit of the Spirit. These character attributes are what the Spirit grows in us. God's grace at work is us produces these attributes in increasing dimensions. A believer ought to be able to sense that they are increasing in their ability to live out these key personal character traits. Am I increasing in my ability to love? Am I more joyful than I was a year ago? Am I more at peace than I used to be?

- Love
- Joy
- Peace
- Patience
- Kindness
- Goodness
- Faithfulness
- Gentleness
- Self-control

Love

Love is first, and that is not an accident. Love is foundational for all of the other attributes that Paul lists. Paul uses derivatives of the term, love, 110 times in his writings! When Paul defines love in 1 Corinthians 13, he includes many of the concepts included in the Fruit of the Spirit. Agape love is not a feeling or emotion. It is not something you "fall into." Love is a deliberate decision to give yourself sacrificially to another.

Joy

Joy is based on the word, grace. Joy is the happy confidence that no matter what happens to you, God is in control and it will all work out to your ultimate, eternal good. You can smile in the midst of difficult days because you know it won't always be like this. Trials and troubles can never steal your inner contentment with God. Paul tells us in Philippians 4, "Rejoice in the Lord always. I will say it again: Rejoice!"

Peace

Peace here is not absence of conflict. Shalom is the Hebrew word that describes a person who is complete, whole, well, and in perfect harmony with God, themselves, and others. Shalom is peace in its deepest sense. It means to be well with God, with ourselves, and with others.

Patience

Patience is the character to wait on God and others without anger and frustration. It is the character to endure situations with grace. How easily we become impatient with other drivers, with our families, or even the checker at the grocery store. Patience is the ability to endure these and even more critical situations.

Kindness

Kindness is the opposite of what the world gives us, "biting, devouring, and consuming one another." Kindness treats even the most casual interchanges with people as important. Others are worthy of our kindness because they are valuable to God.

Goodness

Goodness is the character to "do good to everyone" (Galatians 6:10). Goodness is benevolence and generosity toward others.[49] Goodness is love in action.[50]

---

[49] Timothy George, *Galatians, The New American Commentary* *(Nashville: Broadman, Kindle Edition)*.
[50] Warren Wiersbe, *The BE Series Bundle: Paul's Letters*, (Colorado Springs: David C. Cook, 1977), Kindle Edition.

Faithfulness
Faithfulness is loyalty to God and to others that we love. Faithfulness says, "I'm with you no matter what." Faithfulness keeps its relationships and its promises. Faithfulness is the elderly couple who has weathered the storms of life and marriage. They have survived because they are committed. In the end, there is a holiness and connectedness that comes with living a faithful and true life.

Gentleness
Gentleness is not weakness. The word means "power under control." The word was used in ancient days to describe a powerful stallion who was trained to be completely in control of his strength. Gentleness is power and authority under control. Gentleness rejects power plays and silly inner competitions.

Self-control
Self-control is the ability to overcome our physical and emotional passions and desires, and to respond as the Scripture and the Spirit lead us. Self-control is the ability to do what's right and good even when it's hard.

Years ago, my family traveled with me for a meeting in Lancaster, Pennsylvania. Among the many things we saw was the following print done by Freiman Stoltzfus.[51] In the print we see people whose expressions display the beauty of one transformed by the Spirit of God into right relationship with others. I see that print every day, for it

---

[51] Freiman Stoltzfus, *Fruit of the Spirit*, Freiman Stoltzfus Gallery, www.freimanstoltzfus.com

hangs at the top of the stairs in the entry way of our home. It is a constant reminder of the power of the Holy Spirit to transform me, to change me, and to reflect His goodness and kindness through my life.

Questions for Discussion

1. Is there fruit in your life that gives evidence of God's Spirit at work in you?
2. Are you experiencing personal growth in any of these character attributes?
3. Which areas are the most challenging to you?
4. Do a Bible search on the internet to find Scriptures that deal with the areas in which you need to grow.
5. How might you give the Spirit greater latitude to transform and change you?

Used by permission of the artist, © Freiman Stoltzfus

THE CHURCH IS ABOUT RELATIONSHIPS

Church is not a place that we go to; church is not a building. For way too many people, the church is a place that they go once a week listening to someone they don't know, preach about things they don't understand, with people they don't know. Biblical church is a spiritual family that worships together, supports each other, encourages each other, loves each other, and helps each other live out their faith in real life. The Church is about relationships.

> *Biblical church is a spiritual family that worships together, supports each other, encourages each other, loves each other, and helps each other live out their faith in real life.*

When I was a Kindergartener, we moved to Grand Island, Nebraska to a very small Air Force Base. My family was new to the area and we were looking for connections. One of my dad's fellow airmen invited us to church. My mom, who would have normally resisted, said yes. We started going to church. Some months later, my mom professed faith in Jesus Christ as her Savior and Lord.

Through an elderly Sunday School teacher, I began to understand the Bible. She taught us children's songs that I still teach today. She taught us the Lord's Prayer and the 23rd Psalm. She spoke to us about Jesus. Our family life began to revolve around the church.

When we moved to Billings, Montana, I remember the day that I realized I needed Jesus and understood what He had done for me at the cross. That evening I followed Jesus in believer's baptism. Looking back on it all, that was the day I became united with Christ's Church.

At age eight, I understood and accepted the basics:

- I knew I had sinned against God.
- I knew I deserved punishment for my sin.
- I understand God sent His Son, Jesus to take my punishment upon Himself.
- I believed Jesus died in my place
- I decided to start living in obedience to Jesus' teachings.
- I knew the church would help me grow.

Many people today claim to have faith in Jesus Christ but hate His Church. They accurately notice that the church is full of sinners and hypocrites. I well remember the old bumper sticker, "Christians aren't perfect, just forgiven." That is so true.

I don't think Jesus' disciples knew what was coming until Jesus established His Church in Acts 2. They knew Christ's Spirit was going to come, but how and for what purpose was largely still a mystery. When the Spirit fell on the gathered followers of Jesus Christ, a mighty force was unleased upon the world. Over the next decades the faithful followers of Jesus were martyred proclaiming the truth of the resurrection. Many had seen the resurrected Jesus with their own eyes (1 Corinthians 15), the others had experienced His presence through the Spirit. They were so sure of what they had seen and experienced in the resurrection of Jesus that death was no obstacle to their testimony. Death? So, what! Jesus had already defeated death.

They were so sure of what they had seen and experienced in the resurrection of Jesus that death was no obstacle to their testimony. Death? So, what! Jesus had already defeated death!

At a huge outcropping of rock outside Caesarea Philippi, Jesus told his disciples, "and upon this rock I will build my church" (Matthew 16:18). His disciples were no doubt confused about what Jesus meant, but they understand that there would be a great assembly of people who would come to know Jesus as the Messiah. After the resurrection, the Apostle Paul began to theologically define the church and used several metaphors that give substance to her purpose. Perhaps his strongest metaphor is the Body of Christ (1 Corinthians 12:12-13, 27, Romans 12:4-5, Colossians 1:18, 24).

Caesarea Philippi, The Rock

The Body of Christ

In the Body of Christ (the Church), Christ is the head (Ephesians 5:23) and we are members related to each other: "For just as the body is one and has many parts, and all the parts of that body, though many, are one body—so also is Christ" (1 Corinthians 12:12). Individuals fit into the Body of Christ for the good of the Body, "A manifestation of the Spirit is given to each person for the common good..." (1 Corinthians 12:7). Like the parts of the human body, each of us has a definite role and purpose within the Church. If one part of the body is sick, the whole body functions poorly. For the body to work

216

well, each part must work in tandem with the others (1 Corinthians 12).

Those who have trusted Jesus are part of the Body of Christ. We come under His leadership and we belong to each other. We must properly relate to each other.

The Oneness of the Body

These are days of division, hatred, anger, strife, and polarization. One can divide almost any church immediately with discussions about world view, politics, immigration policy, racism, injustice, sex, or national views on health care. It's easy to provoke disunity.

But only one thing can unite us. Only One person can bring us together and heal us. Only Jesus. Only Jesus can break the power of sin. Only Jesus can free us from our bondage to selfishness. Only Jesus can move us beyond our narrow perspective to see our brother's perspective. Only Jesus.

> *Only Jesus can unite us!*
> *Nothing else can hold us together!*

When we find our unity in Christ, then we have discovered the power of one—the power of the Gospel— the power to change the world. Jesus.

Hours before the cross, Jesus prayed for His disciples and all future believers. He asked the Father to make us one. His request was based on the truth that Jesus and the Father are one. He rooted the basis for our unity in the oneness of the Trinity.

"May they all be one, as You, Father, are in Me and I am in You" (John 17:21). Again, in verse 21, "May they be one as We are one." God the Father is in perfect relationship with the Son. We are to be in perfect relationships with Christ who brings us into perfect relationship with each other.

This prayer is intimately filled with expressions of love between the Son and His Father:

> As you have loved me (23)
> Because you have loved me (24)
> I have known you (25)
> I made your name known... so the love you
>   have loved me with may be in them and I
>   may be in them. (26)

Verse 26, draws us into that circle of love, "so the love you have loved me with may be in them and I may be in them." We were once alienated from God and each other because of sin, but through the cross, Jesus reconciled us to the Father and to each other. He brought us peace!

Isaiah told us this would happen when he prophesied of the cross 700 years before Christ came.

"But He was pierced because of our transgressions, crushed because of our iniquities; punishment for our peace was on Him, and we are healed by His wounds." Isaiah 53:5

Paul went on to write in Ephesians about the dividing wall of hostility between peoples. Christ has torn down the wall! He has made us one.

Since God is at One with Himself, and we are in Christ one with Jesus, then we become one with all others who are one with Jesus. Hear Jesus's words:

> May they all be one. (21)
> May they be one as we are one (22)
> May they be made completely one (23)

There is incredible power in the number: one! Jesus noted in his prayer, that when we display oneness as the people of God then, "the world may know you have sent me and have loved them as you have loved me" (23). When we live out the unity of the Body of Christ, the world will know who Jesus is, the one true and living God. The only one who can heal the divisions between us.

How the Body Works

Romans 12 instructs us about how the church operates. I have frequently preached this passage to show how God plans for the Church to work.

First, God's plan is that we must first die to ourselves to become part of the Body of Christ, "I urge you to present your bodies as a living sacrifice, holy and pleasing to God..." (Romans 12:1). Sin owns us; separated from God we are selfish and self-centered. Life is all about us. When we receive God's forgiveness and commit ourselves to following Jesus, we must die to our old self. Becoming part of the church is about losing ourselves in God and in His plan and purposes.

Secondly, Paul wants us to understand that dying to ourselves is only the beginning. We need to be transformed or changed. Within the church, God's Spirit will take God's Word and God's people and begin to transform us.

> "Do not be conformed to this age, but be transformed by the renewing of your mind, so that you may discern what is the good, pleasing, and perfect will of God" (verse 2).

Christ wants to change us. We cannot change ourselves, but His Spirit will transform us as we yield ourselves to His ways and will. He will use the church to help us on this journey.

Third, we must find our place of service in the church. We must find and engage our gifts and our abilities for the good of others:

> Now as we have many parts in one body, and all the parts do not have the same function, in the same way we who are many are one body in Christ and individually members of one another. According to the grace given to us, we have different gifts: If prophecy, use it according to the proportion of one's faith; if service, use it in service; if teaching, in teaching; if exhorting, in exhortation; giving, with

generosity; leading, with diligence; showing mercy, with cheerfulness. Romans 12:4-8

God's Spirit gives us gifts and abilities to serve each other and the mission of the church. The Spirit gives some administrative abilities to serve. He gives some the ability to encourage, some to teach, some to lead, some to give, some to counsel, some to care, some to minister. The Spirit gives all of us gifts to serve Christ in the church.

Finally, we must learn to live out the second commandment, "love your neighbor as yourself," within the Body of Christ, so that we can live it out in the world around us. We must learn to love through the crucible of life. What Paul gives us in the rest of Romans 12 are the practical challenges and sacrifices of love in action.

> **Let love be without hypocrisy.** Detest evil; cling to what is good. Love one another deeply as brothers and sisters. Take the lead in honoring one another. Do not lack diligence in zeal; be fervent in the Spirit; serve the Lord. Rejoice in hope; be patient in affliction; be persistent in prayer. Share with the saints in their needs; pursue hospitality. Bless those who persecute you; bless and do not curse. Rejoice with those who rejoice; weep with those who weep. Live in harmony with one another. Do not be proud; instead, associate with the humble. Do not be wise in your own estimation. Do not repay anyone evil for evil. Give careful thought to do what is honorable in everyone's eyes. If possible, as far as it depends on you, live at peace with everyone. Friends, do not avenge yourselves; instead, leave room for

God's wrath, because it is written, Vengeance belongs
to me; I will repay, says the Lord. But If your enemy
is hungry, feed him. If he is thirsty, give him
something to drink. For in so doing you will be
heaping fiery coals on his head. Do not be conquered
by evil but conquer evil with good. Romans 12:9-21

What the Body Does

I have often been amazed at how few Christians
understand what the church is supposed to do. Back in
the 1990's Rick Warren became famous for his book, *The
Purpose Driven Church*. I read it and was amazed that it
was simply the expanded outline of one of my very first
days of seminary in a class on religious education. Warren
had taken the patterns of the Acts 2 church and applied
them to our modern day by building them into a new
church.

Acts 2:41-47 is crucial to understanding what the church
is supposed to do:

So those who accepted his message were baptized,
and that day about three thousand people were added
to them. They devoted themselves to the apostles'
teaching, to the fellowship, to the breaking of bread,
and to prayer. Everyone was filled with awe, and
many wonders and signs were being performed
through the apostles. Now all the believers were
together and held all things in common. They sold
their possessions and property and distributed the
proceeds to all, as any had need. Every day they
devoted themselves to meeting together in the

temple, and broke bread from house to house. They ate their food with joyful and sincere hearts, praising God and enjoying the favor of all the people. Every day the Lord added to their number those who were being saved.
Acts 2:41-47

From this snapshot of the early church, pastors typically identify no less than five functions of the church: worship, evangelism, discipleship, fellowship, and ministry. These are the things that the church is supposed to do!

1. Worship
Worship is about loving, adoring, marveling, focusing, praising, listening to, and responding to God! Worship is about our relationship with God.

2. Evangelism
Evangelism is telling others about Jesus' incarnation, life, death, and resurrection and inviting them into a relationship with Jesus. Evangelism is sharing the good news that God wants to heal us of our brokenness and forgive us of all our sin.

3. Discipleship
Discipleship is teaching others the Word of God and helping them to personally grow through the power of the Word and the Spirit. Discipleship is about becoming a new person in Christ. Discipleship is about helping others grow in their relationship with Jesus and each other.

4. Fellowship

Fellowship is about sharing life and caring for one another within the Body of Christ. Fellowship is enjoying the enrichment that others bring to our lives. Fellowship is about relationship.

5. Ministry

Ministry is about sharing God's love through meeting the needs of others. Ministry is about caring for people in tangible ways. It's offering a "cold cup of water in Jesus' name." It's about offering a listening ear and biblical wisdom. It's about writing a check when someone needs assistance. Ministry is about relationships.

The Sanctifying Power of the Church

Someone once said, "The church is like Noah's ark: The stench inside would be unbearable if it weren't for the storm outside."

I know that church life can occasionally be tough. I have served the church for over thirty years and have seen people at their worst. Horrible things are occasionally done by church people. Some people who lead churches may not even have a genuine relationship with Jesus, some have simply lost their way. They were never taught to live out the teachings of the Bible or were never held accountable for bad behavior. They probably never received loving correction and accountability.

But here's the thing—the majority of people I work with today are good and gracious people trying to live out their faith! They are trying to the best of their abilities to

224

love God and love people. In the last decade, I see fewer and fewer conflicts and less judgmentalism in the church. I see the camaraderie of fellow sinners helping each other live the goodness of the Christian life. I am much encouraged.

> *I see fewer and fewer conflicts and less judgmentalism in the church.*
> *I see the authentic camaraderie of fellow sinners helping each other live the goodness of the Christian life.*
> *I am much encouraged!*

Christ founded the church as the place where His followers would find encouragement and strength to follow Jesus. The church is the place where we can find weekly encouragement, "Therefore encourage one another and build each other up, just as in fact you are doing" (1 Thessalonians 5:11).

The church is the place where we "Bear with each other and forgive one another if any of you has a grievance against someone. Forgive as the Lord forgave you" (Colossians 3:13).

The church is where we learn what's right and wrong. The church is where we get support when we fail. The church is where we learn to get along with people who are different than us. The church is our spiritual family.

Our brothers and sisters help us grow stronger as we learn to live through life's challenges and struggles. The church is the hospital for sinners recovering from sin, being ministered to by each other, learning to walk in the grace of God.

Leadership Development in the Church

Too many people think that leadership is about the power to tell people what to do. Real leadership is about the ability to cooperate together for a greater good. Leadership is less about power and more about relationship. The church plays a key role in the development of Christian leaders.

My college pastor, Tom Bray helped develop me by giving me the opportunity to teach the High School boys Sunday School class. Later he recommended that I be the chairman of the personnel committee for our church at only 21 years of age. When I felt the call to ministry, Brother Tom looked up at me and said, "I wondered how long it would take you to see this." He had been working for years to raise me up and equip me as a leader. He became my father in the ministry and was instrumental in guiding me to seminary, to my first church, and then through ordination. He helped develop me into a leader.

When I answered my next call to our second church in Sioux City, Iowa, I felt a thousand miles away from any support. But in the third year we called a new associational missionary to our region. Mark Elliott became that mentor and influence in my life. Frequently, we talked through challenges and ministry. His friendship and mentorship made me better and still does to this day.

In my tenth year of ministry in northern Iowa, I was president of the Baptist Convention of Iowa during a transition period in which the old executive director had retired, and a new executive director was called. It was a challenging time and I learned a great deal. The convention called Jimmy Barrentine to lead us. Jimmy became a friend and a mentor for me. It was his affirmation that encouraged me to take the seemingly impossible step of becoming the executive director of the Minnesota-Wisconsin Baptist Convention. In my earliest days in this role, Jimmy was my example. He taught me how to lead at a new level.

In these last sixteen years God has provided another friend and mentor who has taught me, guided me, and sharpened me in ways I could not have imagined. My predecessor, Bill Tinsley, has regularly injected into my thinking new ideas about life and ministry. He has sharpened me and encouraged me. He has taught me the power of listening and reflecting. One of the greatest things Bill has taught me is the power of letting people tell their stories. It is amazing how quickly people can build a lasting connection when they listen to each other. He has enriched my life and sharpened my relationship skills. He has made me a better leader.

If I am useful in the Kingdom of God today, it is to a large degree because of the influence of these leaders who built relationships with me, invested in me, and called out the best in me. They were the church leaders that

God used to develop in me the ability to lead. Leadership is about relationships.

I have tried to pass on what I have learned by mentoring high school seniors, church planters, pastors, students, and leaders. What I have discovered is that it's not really about the process, the perimeters, or giving the right answer. It's about all about relationships.

Questions for Discussion

1. What would you say to a person who says, "I believe in God, but not in the church?"
2. What does "the Body of Christ" mean?
3. Are you a member of a church? Why or why not?
4. How has the church failed you?
5. What is a church supposed to do?
6. What is your role in the church?
7. Who were the leaders that influenced you, taught you, and mentored you to new levels of growth?

PEACE IS ABOUT RELATIONSHIPS

The National Alliance of Mental Illness reports that 19.1 percent of American adults live with anxiety disorders.[52] A recent study in the journal of Psychophysiology notes that "loving relationships are associated with less stress, less physiologic reactivity and even a longer lifespan."[53] Relationships have the potential to bring us peace.

In the Middle East today people greet one another by briefly connecting relationally with a word that combines acknowledgement, greeting, and blessing. They say, "Shalom." The word technically means peace, but when spoken between two individuals there is a deep underlying understanding that peace comes in the blessed relationship between people.

---

[52] National Alliance of Mental Illness, "Anxiety Disorders", December 2017, https://www.nami.org/About-Mental-Illness/Mental-Health-Conditions/Anxiety-Disorders
[53] Jack Turban, Psychology Today: "The mental Image of a Loved One Can Keep Down Blood Pressure", January 23, 2019. https://www.psychologytoday.com/us/blog/political-minds/201901/the-mental-image-loved-one-can-keep-down-blood-pressure

Most of us hunger for peace. Good relationships have the potential to bring us real peace. Biblical peace begins in our relationship with God and then is extended to the people around us. One who does not have the peace of God can hardly share peace with another.

J. Oswald Sanders captures this well, "Peace is not the absence of trouble, but the presence of God." The closer we get to God the more we will experience His peace, and the more we can share it with another.

> [It is] Essential for us to understand that peace with God precedes peace with others. "A man who is at war with himself will be at war with others."
> --Dag Hammerskjold

I'm a type A personality. I'm not programed to sit still and do nothing. I do, do, do. Peace is hard for me, yet I still long for it. The most relaxed I ever feel is when I'm sipping coffee with God or my family and friends. Their presence brings me peace.

I find it interesting that at the birth of Jesus the announcement of the angels focused on the glory of God and our peace.

> "And suddenly there was with the angel a multitude of the heavenly host praising God and saying, "Glory to God in the highest, and on earth peace among those with whom he is pleased" (Luke 2:13).

We are to imitate the announcement. We are to give glory to God, and when we do, God brings peace to man.

The LORD God of Israel desired for His people to experience His peace. He called upon the religious leaders of the Old Testament to bless His people with the words of Numbers 6:24-16.

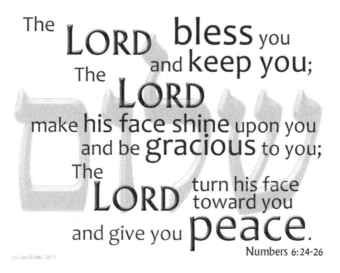

The LORD bless you
The and keep you;
LORD
make his face shine upon you
and be gracious to you;
The
LORD turn his face
toward you
and give you peace.

(c) Leo Endel 2011

Numbers 6:24-26

Shalom, the Hebrew word for peace, is a rich and meaningful word. It means to be whole, to be complete, to live in a state of wholeness and well-being, happiness, prosperity, health, completeness, security and safety.

Peace comes when we learn to trust God, "The steadfast of mind You will keep in perfect peace, because he trusts in You." Isaiah 26:3

Jesus said in John 16:33, "I have told you these things so that in me you may have peace." Notice carefully that we experience peace in Christ! In our relationship with Jesus we experience peace. "You will have suffering in this world. Be courageous! I have conquered the world" (John 16:33).

Our peace is ultimately found in Christ. "For He is our peace…" (Ephesians 2:14). He is both our peace with God and with each other. We find our peace in a relationship with Jesus; we bring that peace to others in our personal relationships.

Jesus is our peace:

- **Jesus is the means through which we can have peace with God.** He ended the hostility between our sinfulness and God's purity when He paid the penalty for our sin at the cross.

- **Jesus is the means through which we can have inner peace.** He begins to transform our inner sinfulness and brokenness so we might be at peace within our own spirit.

- **Jesus is the means through which we can have peace with each other.** Jesus transforms our character so that we respond to others in love rather than through our inner brokenness, judgmentalism, anger, jealousy, and frustration.

Paul picks up on this truth in Colossians 3:15, "Let the peace of Christ rule in your hearts…" All of Paul's letters begin with words of blessing like these, "Grace and peace to you from God our Father and the Lord Jesus Christ." Paul knew there was no real and lasting peace but through the peace of Jesus Christ.

Augustine said of God, "Thou has made us for yourself, and the heart of man is restless until it finds rest in You." Find your rest, find your peace in Jesus.

Questions for Discussion

1. Are you at peace with God?
2. On a scale of 1 (no anxiety to 10 (great anxiety), what is your level of anxiety?
3. Are you at peace with your family and friends?
4. What could you do to become a person of peace among your family, friends, neighbors, and work associates?
5. In what ways is Jesus our peace?

BLESSING IS ABOUT RELATIONSHIPS

As we have just seen, God desires for His people to be blessed. He commanded the Aaronic priests to pronounce a blessing over His people on a regular basis.

I grew up an evangelical reactionary to Catholicism. When my mom and dad married, they married in a marriage chapel in Las Vegas. My mom's hometown priest offered to bless their marriage and my dad refused the blessing—I don't know if he said what he was thinking or not, but his background taught that no man could bless others in this way. To some degree, he was right; to another degree, he was wrong.

Certainly, we would all agree that offering a prayer on behalf of another is a blessing. Modern translations make this truth clear by adding what is explicitly understood from the text by adding the word, "May" to the blessing. In this way the blessing is clearly a request for God to bless.

May the LORD bless you and protect you;
May the LORD make his face shine on you
And be gracious to you;
May the LORD look with favor on you
And give you peace.
Numbers 6:24-26

This simple adjustment reminds us that we can indeed become "channels of blessing" to the people around us. Let us not forget that Peter says we are now a kingdom of priests (1 Peter 2:5, 9). We are authorized to pronounce the blessing! The Apostle Paul does a shortened version of the blessing in almost all of his letters, "Grace and peace from God our Father and the Lord Jesus Christ." He was passing on the blessing.

We can share the blessing of God with people around us by praying God's blessing on them. The  best way to bless people is to pray with them in person, but many nights I pray blessings on the people God brings to my mind. I fall asleep passing on the blessing! If you are my Facebook friend, you will likely receive Numbers 6:24-26 from me on your birthday. I literally pray this verse for you and then post it on your Facebook page. I am praying that God will bless you!

Years ago, I read John Trent and Gary Smalley's book, *The Blessing*. I was moved by the Scriptural legacy and personal stories of people impacted through the blessing of others. Ultimately, I attempted to bless people as broadly as possible with prayer and words of affirmation.

First, I wrote a tribute to my wife, framed it in a beautiful frame and gave it to her for our anniversary. Then, sometime later, I wrote one for my mom. Occasionally, I pause and read these expressions of appreciation, praise, and prayer. They are truer today than the day I wrote them. I attempt to live out these blessings through ongoing words and deeds of love. Soon I plan to write blessings for both of my girls, Rachel and Lydia.

In a world of incredible negativity, criticism and judgmentalism, healing words are powerful. I want to leave a legacy to people who have experienced encouragement and affirmation from my lips. I want people to know that I love them. I want them to know they have impacted my life. I want them to know that I pray for them. I want them to know that God desires to bless them. I want God to make me a blessing to them.

Questions for Discussion:

1. What is a blessing?
2. Who can bless?
3. Who has blessed you?
4. Who should you bless?
5. How could you practice loving your family and friends through sharing a blessing?

IRISH Blessing

May the Road
Rise to meet you;
May the wind be always
at your back,
May the sun shine warm
upon your face,
and the Rain fall soft
upon your fields,
and until we meet again,
May God hold you
in the hollow of his hand.

In loving memory
of my grandmother
Catherine McHugh Wilson

237

HEAVEN IS ABOUT RELATIONSHIPS

In the Rolling Stone magazine, Stephen King was asked, "Do you want to go to heaven?" He responded:

> I don't want to go to the heaven that I learned about when I was a kid. To me, it seems boring. The idea that you're going to lounge around on a cloud all day and listen to guys play harps? I don't want to listen to harps. I want to listen to Jerry Lee Lewis!"[54]

The biblical heaven is almost completely misunderstood. Who wants to sit around in heaven and play a harp for eternity? I too, think that would get pretty boring!

Here's the great thing about heaven. Finally, we will be perfectly right in our relationship with God and with each other. We will completely and perfectly be all that God created us to be.

---

[54] Andy Greene, "Stephen King: The Rolling Stone Interview", Rolling Stone, October 31, 2014.
https://www.rollingstone.com/culture/culture-features/stephen-king-the-rolling-stone-interview-191529/

In heaven:

- we will experience the constant presence and relationship with God in Christ (Rev 21:3-4).
- We will enjoy perfect relationships with others.
- We will experience the physically perfect heaven in bodies that will never grow old, hurt, or decay.
- We will experience abundance and delight (Revelation 22:2).
- We will experience perfect peace (Revelation 21:4).

> *Your best day on earth will not measure up to a single day in heaven.*

This is the new heaven and the new earth. The first earth was "good." Could it be that the new heaven and the new earth are like our current heaven and earth only perfect? Perfect in relationships. Perfect in happiness, excitement, creativity, fulfillment, satisfaction, health/wellness, peace. Could it be that all we long for is this life is ultimately fulfilled in the next? This all seems consistent with the heart of God in His original creation.

What if every experience in heaven is better than any experience we had on this fallen earth? We would be giving up nothing and gaining everything! This world is beautiful, imagine what the next will look like. Will there be animals in heaven? I believe they will be there. They were part of God's original good creation—why wouldn't He include them in heaven. Isaiah 11:65 says, "wolf will dwell with the lamb, leopard will lie down with the goat."

I love the old song by Keith Green,

> I can't wait to get to heaven,
> You'll wipe away all my fears.
> In six days, You created everything,
> but You've been working on heaven
> two thousand years.[55]

And we will reign forever and ever (Revelation 22:4). We were given our place to care for creation in this world (Genesis 2:15), heaven will have a place from which we will serve God, each other, and His creation too. We will be fulfilled in our role and rewarded with joy and fulfillment. In everything we do, we will worship the goodness and glory of God.

You'll have a job in heaven just like Adam had a job in the Garden of Eden, but it will not be toil, it will be full of joy and meaning. Your work will cause the rest of us to constantly praise God for His glory reflected in you and in God's new heaven.

---

[55] Keith Green, "I Can't Wait to Get to Heaven," from the Prodigal Son Album, The Universal Music Group, https://www.youtube.com/watch?v=_gotfop41dc

What if today's artist or the lighting director gets to plan, orchestrate, and develop her own sunsets while we ooh and ahh like at a fireworks show?

What if today's florist or gardener gets to plant and maintain an entire hillside and crossbreed new colors or varieties that we can't even imagine today?

What if today's scientist discovers and then teaches us the glory of God's incredible design behind creation so that we can praise the infinite wisdom and creativity of God?

What if today's actors and writers write plays that so honor God and reveal His glory that we break out in spontaneous praise and worship? Movies in the garden every night, books to read by the evening campfires, will delight us forever.

What if today's musicians write songs with harmonies and sounds that will so amaze us that we are immediately moved to worship the LORD? And then in their glorious praise we are led before the throne in morning and evening worship, the multitudes of all the ages giving praise and honor to God.

What is to keep us from destroying the new heaven and the new earth with new sin? All of us who have trusted and believed in Jesus will remember what it was like to live in a broken world. We will have drunk the sewer water of sin and suffered in this broken world. When we receive the cool refreshing living water of God we will never go back to the sewer. We will never again doubt the goodness of God (Genesis 3). We will know for eternity that there is no good thing apart from God.

We will live forever in perfect relationship with God and with each other. "The throne of God and of the Lamb will be in the city" and we "will serve him." "And we will reign for ever and ever" (Revelation 22:5).

C.S. Lewis ends the Chronicles of Narnia, in heaven, with Aslan (the Christ figure) explaining to Peter, Susan, Edmund, and Lucy, what had happened to them in the Shadowlands, and where they now reside.

> "'There was a railway accident,' said Aslan softly. 'Your father and mother and all of you are, as you used to call it in the Shadowlands, dead. The term is over, the holidays have begun. The dream is ended; this is the morning.'

> "As he spoke, he no longer appeared to them like a lion, but the things that began to happen after that were so great and beautiful that I cannot write them. For us this is the end of all the stories, and we can most truly say that they all lived happily ever after; but for them it was only the beginning of the real story. All their lives in this world and all their adventures in Narnia had only been the cover and the title page. Now, at last, they were beginning Chapter One of the great story, which no one on earth has read, which goes on forever, in which every chapter is better than the one before."[56]

---

[56] C. S. Lewis, *The Chronicles of Narnia: The Last Battle*, (Harper Collins: New York, 1994), 228.

Questions for Discussion

1. What do you think heaven will be like?
2. What does God's original creation tell us about heaven?
3. What do you think about the concept of work in heaven?
4. What might be your occupation in heaven?
5. Why won't we sin in heaven?
6. How sure are you that you will be in heaven?

THE FINAL CHAPTER
THE GOOD SAMARITAN

Nearly everyone knows Jesus' parable of the Good Samaritan. The story is so powerful that most of us know the question raised by the lawyer, "Who is my neighbor?" We also know the answer, "everyone is my neighbor." But most of us have forgotten the original question asked by the lawyer, "What must I do to inherit eternal life?" Jesus's powerful story answers both questions (Luke 10:30-37).

"A man was going down from Jerusalem to Jericho and fell into the hands of robbers. They stripped him, beat him up, and fled, leaving him half dead. A priest happened to be going down that road. When he saw him, he passed by on the other side. In the same way, a Levite, when he arrived at the place and saw him, passed by on the other side. But a Samaritan on his journey came up to him, and when he saw the man, he had compassion. He went over to him and bandaged his wounds, pouring on olive oil and wine. Then he put him on his own animal, brought him to an inn, and took care of him. The next day he took out two denarii, gave them to the innkeeper, and said, 'Take care of him. When I come back, I'll reimburse you for whatever extra you spend.' "Which of these three do you think proved to be a neighbor to the man who fell into the hands of the robbers?" "The one who showed mercy to him," he said. Then Jesus told him, "Go and do the same."

"What must I do to inherit eternal life?" The man gives the right answer, "love God and love others." But knowing he hasn't done this perfectly, he asks a second question looking for the legal loophole, "Who is my neighbor?" Jesus' story makes it clear that everyone— even the most despised outcast is still our neighbor. The lawyer's hopes are dashed—there is no loophole. He has not fulfilled the justice of the law of love; presumably, he will not inherit eternal life.

BUT, Jesus' story provides a liberating answer to our guilty friend and to each of us. If we switch our roles within the parable, Jesus' answer is astonishing.[57] Put yourself in the place of the wounded, bleeding man lying in the road, broken by sin, religion, and the law. See Jesus as the Good Samaritan who sees our brokenness (v33), comes to us in compassion, saves us (v33), pays the price for our sin (v34-35), and is coming again to give us eternal life (v35)!

"What must I do to inherit eternal life?" Absolutely nothing! Jesus saves us and gives us, by grace, eternal life! Simply, allow Him to save you. Eternal life is all about relationships. Find your life in Jesus!

---

[57] As did most of the early church Fathers: Riemer Roukema, JSTOR, "The Good Samaritan in Ancient Christianity", 2004.

ABOUT THE AUTHOR

Leo Endel was born in Tampa, Florida into a tight knit Air Force family that moved six months later to Anchorage, Alaska. Before graduating from high school, they moved ten more times living in Kansas, Nebraska, Missouri, Montana, Nevada, Alaska (again), Upper Michigan, California, the Philippines and finally back to Missouri.

Leo is a Business Administration graduate of the University of Central Missouri where he received the Wall Street Journal Award in recognition of outstanding academic achievement in Finance. He received his master's degree from Southwestern Baptist Theological Seminary, and his doctorate from Midwestern Baptist Theological Seminary where his dissertation was recognized as the top research project of the Southern Baptist Convention in 2012. In 2014, he was named Midwestern Seminary's Alumnus of the Year.

Dr. Endel has pastored in Leeton, Missouri and Sioux City, Iowa. Additionally, he has done interim pastorates in Minnesota and Wisconsin. He is now serving as the senior pastor of Emmanuel Baptist Church in Rochester, Minnesota and as the Executive Director of the Minnesota-Wisconsin Baptist Convention. Additionally, he teaches doctoral classes in leadership for Midwestern Baptist Theological Seminary. He is the author of "Where Do We Go from Here: Strategic Planning for the Smaller Church."

He and his wife Sarah live in Rochester, Minnesota with their two dogs, Stella and Bailey, and have two grown daughters: Rachel, who lives in St. Louis, and Lydia who lives just south of Honolulu. His wife, Sarah, teaches mathematics at the Rochester Community and Technical College and online mathematics for Spurgeon College, Kansas City, Missouri.

Made in the USA
Monee, IL
24 November 2020